Hospitality & Restaurant Design

Roger Yee

No. 3

HOSPITALITY & RESTAURANT DESIGN

ROGER YEE   NO. 3

Visual Reference Publications Inc., New York

Left: Orchid Lounge Royal Pacific Hotel, Orlando, FL
Architect: Fugleberg Koch Architects, Winter Park, FL
Interior Design: Daroff Design, Philadelphia, PA
Photography: Peter Page.

Visual Reference Publications, Inc.
302 Fifth Avenue
New York, NY 10001

Distributors to the trade in the United States and Canada
Watson-Guptill
770 Broadway
New York, NY 10003

Distributors outside the United States and Canada
HarperCollins International
10 East 53 Street
New York, NY 10022-5299

Book Design: Harish Patel Design Associates, New York
Book Production: John Hogan

Library of Congress Cataloging in Publication Data:
Hospitality & Restaurant Design No.3
Printed in China
ISBN 1-58471-068-3

Contents

Introduction

What could be more implausible or delightful than a bevy of beautiful young women in white evening gowns, seated at white grand pianos that sweep effortlessly across a vast ballroom floor in long, serpentine lines? The scene comes out of the Warner Brothers musical Gold Diggers of 1935, directed by Busby Berkeley, and it's a reminder that people enjoy dining out, traveling and entertainment even in troubled times. Indeed, this is why the hospitality industry is moving beyond the difficulties of recent years by unveiling new, imaginative and appealing services—plus irresistible environments where we can experience them.

As the pages of Hospitality & Restaurant Design No. 3 reveal, hoteliers and restaurateurs are catering to our desire for escape with environments that seem more attractive, comfortable and intriguing than our homes and workplaces could ever be. At the Grand Resort Lagonissi in Athens, for example, DiLeonardo International has designed the Kohylia Restaurant & Sushi Bar to offer a Polynesian and Japanese fantasy in a Mediterranean environment for a Greek hotel. A different imagery enlivens the St. Regis Shanghai, where HBA/Hirsch Bedner Associates has transformed the triple-height lobby into what could easily be mistaken for a contemporary theater or opera house, and is now one of the most popular meeting places in town.

Yet many of us are not pining for Shangri-La as much as a glorified version of our own, familiar world. In fact, numerous hotels and restaurants succeed by celebrating the historic and cultural roots of their communities. Consider how Fort Worth's cowboy heritage, based on the great cattle drives on the Chisholm Trail, has helped make an overnight success of the Chisholm Club, a restaurant designed by Arnold Syrop Associates to resemble a gracious Texas ranch house. Similarly, BAR Architects has drawn on California's beloved Craftsman style of the early 20th century to invest the new clubhouse of the Sharon Heights Golf and Country Club, in Menlo Park, with the spirit of the building it replaced.

Of course, being a good hotelier or restaurateur involves more than hiring the right designer to develop a winning scheme. Today's customers demand value, comfort and convenience, and hoteliers are learning to be friendly to families arriving for weekend stays after business meetings, women traveling on business, and corporate travelers trying to save money. Restaurateurs are adding less expensive entrees to menus and introducing healthier fare, exotic cuisines and take-out to encourage guests to dine out as often as possible.

Still, presentation counts heavily in the end, and Hospitality & Restaurant Design No. 3 shows how some of today's leading architects and interior designers are tempting us to leave our cocoons. As an added service to readers, we have identified the key sources of building products and furnishings used in their projects. Now, any search for the best resources to develop hotels and restaurants can begin in our pages, drawing on these key sources and information from our participating sponsors.

Welcome to Hospitality & Restaurant Design No. 3. Your place is waiting.

Roger Yee
Editor

Aria Group Architects, Inc.

830 North Boulevard
Oak Park, IL 60301
708.445.8400
708.445.1788 (Fax)
www.ariainc.com

Aria Group Architects, Inc.

Aria Group Architects, Inc.

P.F. Chang's China Bistro
Orem, Utah

Above: Table-for-two setting.

Below: Main dining room.

Opposite: Entry tower in a shopping mall.

Photography: Proavis/J. Pyle.

East meets West in the Orem, Utah branch of P.F. Chang's China Bistro, a thriving, Scottsdale, Arizona-based restaurant chain that shrewdly combines Chinese cuisine with such touches as attentive service, wine and tempting desserts, all served in a stylish, high-energy bistro setting. The 180-seat, 5,134-square foot, one-level restaurant, the smallest of numerous P.F. Chang's designed by Aria Group Architects along with Brian Stubstad, P.F. Chang's director of design and architecture, draws customers to its exotic fare through a monumental entry tower with a soaring, two-tiered ceiling, inviting patio, fashionably upholstered banquettes and booths, timeless wood tables and chairs, and a warm palette of golds and reds. For dishes such as Mongolian beef, Shanghai cucumbers and garlic noodles, P.F. Chang's serves the perfect accompaniment.

Aria Group Architects, Inc.

Kona Grill
Kansas City, Missouri

What's a diner averse to eating raw fish to do when everyone else wants sushi? Head for Kona Grill. Growing numbers of customers are giving the Scottsdale, Arizona-based concept fresh opportunities to serve its distinctive menu of contemporary American cuisine, spiced with Hawaiian accents and highlighted by fresh sushi, fresh seafood/steaks, salads, noodle dishes and pizzas. At this location, a 222-seat, 7,240-square foot, one-level space in Kansas City's historic Country Club Plaza, designed by Aria Group Architects, a dynamic oceanic theme is sustained by salt water aquariums, custom lighting fixtures, stone, mahogany and a box-within-a-box layout ideal for people watching whether you love sushi or not.

Aria Group Architects, Inc.

Keefer's
Chicago, Illinois

If Chicago's best steakhouses are temples for carnivores of the city Carl Sandburg called "hog butcher to the world," it's not surprising that Keefer's Restaurant is drawing devotees en masse. The new, 8,000-square foot, 275-seat establishment in a modern office building at 20 West Kinzie, designed by Aria Group Architects, gives noted chef John Hogan an interior to match his acclaimed cuisine of prime steaks, fresh seafood, pasta, chicken and chops. The spacious, contemporary interior revolves in layers like rings of Saturn around a circular bar, using soffits, walls, and open grillwork to accent the geometry. Its decor, which includes such comforting elements as wood tables and chairs, upholstered booths, fireplace, wool carpet, granite, terrazzo, glass tile, table lamps and vintage radios, regularly shares

praise with the menu in the pages of Chicago Magazine, Chicago Tribune, Conde Nast Traveler and Esquire.

Above: Bar and glass store-front.

Left: Diningroom behind bar.

Opposite top: Storefront exterior.

Opposite middle: Dining room facing the street.

Opposite bottom: Dining room flanking bar.

Photography: Mark Ballogg, Steinkamp/Ballogg Chicago.

Aria Group Architects, Inc.

Rumba
Chicago, Illinois

Left: Bar.

Above: Private dining room.

Below: Dining area with booths.

Photography: Doug Snower Photography.

The latest sign that Chicago moves to a Latin beat is Rumba, a reflection of 1950's Cuba with a raised stage for live Latin jazz and dancing that's attracting crowds of thirty-somethings. The 6,500-square foot, 240-seat space, which features red upholstered booths replete with conga drums, mustard walls and a wood-beam ceiling, was designed by Aria Group Architects. Good flow and sightlines showcase chef Israel Calderon's Nuevo Latino Mexican cuisine--and nightly proof Chicagoans really can rumba.

Arnold Syrop Associates, Architects

290 Fifth Avenue
New York, NY 10001
212.947.7070
212.643.8449 (Fax)
arnoldsyrop@arnoldsyrop.com

Arnold Syrop Associates, Architects

Arnold Syrop Associates, Architects

New York Marriott Marquis Atrium
New York, New York

Standing in the cavernous, 41-story New York Marriott Marquis Atrium, you can almost hear Frank Sinatra declaring, "If I can make it there, I can make it anywhere. It's up to you, New York, New York!" It takes a powerful interior design to tame a 32,500-square foot open space, and that's exactly what the New York Marriott Marquis got from Arnold Syrop Associates, which provided architecture and interior

design services, as well as custom-designed furniture, lighting fixtures and graphics. When Host Marriott, owner of the Marriott Marquis, asked the architecture firm for fresh ideas, the Atrium was showing its age. The updating of the space, originally designed by John Portman in 1985, has given it a compelling axial circulation plan and four food service venues with strong and appealing personalities of their own. The

need for good spatial orientation is obvious to anyone who has navigated this sprawling environment, so the new scheme charts a clear path from the circular elevator bank in the center of the Atrium to the perimeter windows overlooking Times Square, New York's fabled entertainment district. Acting as the jewel in this crown is the Atrium Lounge, whose clock tower and spiraling arms, majestically modeled in wood,

LED lighting and mirrors with custom designed lounge furniture, evoke a townhouse living room and act as the pinwheel around which everything revolves. By contrast, the Sushi Bar, reached by a bridge of black granite with a custom designed mosaic of fish and waves is as sharp and snappy as a nightclub with its onyx bar, gleaming steel barstools, black granite tables, red lanterns and sleek waterfalls. A more casual, cafe-like ambiance is established at Encore, the hotel's three-meal restaurant, which welcomes guests to tables and banquettes within sight of a mural depicting the history of live theater. And what could be closer to the action in Times Square than the two-tiered Broadway Lounge, whose swirling curves, traced by banquettes with custom textiles and carpet, entice guests to view the Great White Way?

Left: Encore.
Below: Waterfall at Sushi Bar.
Opposite left: Seating at Clock Lounge.
Opposite lower left: Broadway Lounge beneath chandeliers.

Arnold Syrop Associates, Architects

The Chisholm Club
Renaissance Worthington Hotel
Fort Worth, Texas

Left: Main dining room and open kitchen.

Above: Bar and entrance

Photography: Peter Paige

Cowboy heritage is serious business in Fort Worth, which proudly remembers the great cattle drives that delivered beef from the Chisholm Trail to America's dining tables. Not only does "Cowtown" have its own, official longhorn herd, it also boasts a bumper crop of restaurants offering exceptional Texan and Mexican fare. However, Fort Worth took notice when award-winning chef Grady Spears recently teamed up with the city's finest hotel, the Renaissance Worthington, to create The Chisholm Club, a 7,800-square foot, 208-seat (plus 100-seat private dining) restaurant and cooking school designed by Arnold Syrop Associates. Spears's "cowboy" cuisine with a contemporary twist was the primary draw, of course. Yet guests also complimented the handsome interior design, which stands out from the crowd by evoking a contemporary Texas ranch house. After visiting various examples in the region, Syrop has created a memorable environment featuring such authentic details as wood ceiling trusses, limestone-clad columns, alabaster lighting pendants, ceramic-tiled fireplace, wood wainscoting studded with zinc stars, wood strip floors, wood bar, custom-designed furnishings and regional decor that makes no apologies for celebrating cowboys, cattle ranching or the age of steam-powered railroads. Guests feel welcome as soon as they arrive. The wood bar, accented by

Above left: Ceramic-tiled fireplace.

Above right: Banquette seating beneath a genre painting.

Below: Dining areas marked by level changes and open railings.

uplighted glass shelves and an alabaster counter with embossed copper bullnose, leads them from the entrance to the main dining room and open kitchen, a stainless steel showcase for Texas cooking. No matter where guests sit, they experience the dual sensation of joining a large, convivial gathering as well as being part of an intimate group, thanks to Syrop's careful planning and his use of raised dining platforms. It's a delectable setting for Fort Worth to enjoy such temptations as prime dry-aged beef ribeye, piloncilla rubbed sea bass, and braised duck a lupe.

Austin•Kuester

300 Montgomery Street
Suite 202
Alexandria, VA 22314
703.836.0373
703.836.7254 (Fax)
sakues@aol.com

Austin•Kuester

Austin•Kuester

On Stage Cleveland
Cleveland, Ohio

Cleveland's Rock and Roll Hall of Fame is so successful it has attracted recording artists and other celebrities as well the public since opening in 1995. So when HMS Host asked Austin-Kuester to renovate a 1,400-square foot, 120-seat bar at Cleveland International Airport as On Stage Cleveland, the designers evoked the Hall to make customers feel they're entering a sound stage. People of all ages spot the silver-paneled exterior and stay to enjoy a lively space highlighted by a guitar-shaped bar, metal truss ceiling for stage equipment, 20-foot long fiber optic guitar used as signage, and a sound system that's played "a little too loud."

Above: Exterior.

Below left: Corridor window.

Below right: Guitar-shaped bar.

Opposite: Environmental graphic treatment.

Photography: Hoachlander Davis Photography

Austin•Kuester Hershey's Chocolate World
Hershey, Pennsylvania

Hershey's Chocolate World, the visitors center of Hershey Foods Corporation in Hershey, Pennsylvania, now offers a delectable experience for families who like chocolate. The 35,000-square foot facility, designed by Austin-Kuester to handle 20,000 visitors daily, begins where the Chocolate-Making Tour Ride ends. Having passed through a simulated factory where a cocoa bean from the tropics mixes with milk from a dairy cow in Pennsylvania to become Hershey's chocolate milk, visitors enter a "rural village" of small shops and open barns filled with Hershey's products. From here, they circle a huge planter of banana palms and cocoa bean trees that introduces a "tropical paradise" and marks the transition from retailing to food service. The centerpiece of this "paradise," a giant, tent-like structure, hovers over a common seating area that is encircled by speciality food and beverage concepts. The seating area is surrounded by all Hershey concepts.

Above: Common seating area.

Opposite upper left: "Village fountain" displaying soft toys.

Opposite lower left: Serving stations for some of the various food and beverage concepts.

29

Austin•Kuester

Woodford Reserve Bar and Grill
Louisville, Kentucky

Above left: Bar.

Above right: Restaurant.

Below: Seating group with casks.

Opposite: Lounge area.

Photography: Hoachlander Davis Photography.

Good bourbon takes time. Yet Woodford Reserve has swiftly become the leading super-premium brand in Kentucky, the home of bourbon, outselling more established rivals. Accordingly, HMS Host and Labrot & Graham Distillery commissioned Austin-Kuester to design a 3,200-square foot, 160-seat restaurant/bar at Louisville International Airport as a public showcase for its bourbon. In this evocative setting, drawn from the design of the distillery's late 19th- and early 20th-century buildings and appointed in overstuffed sofas and chairs, custom rugs, wrought iron lamps and other classic furnishings, Woodford Reserve and steak make a perfect match.

Austin•Kuester

Casa Bacardi
Tampa, Florida

Typical airport bars are dark refuges that conceal customers. That's not the image Bacardi and HMS Host were looking for with this new Casa Bacardi Bar located in the Tampa International Airport. This 4,000 square foot facility, designed by Austin Kuester is light and airy with the sparkle of excitement that Bacardi associates with its products and Cuban heritage. On the outside, a curving corrugated metal canopy gives the entry a brilliance, intensified by the floor-to-ceiling glass wall enclosing the bar, that welcomes men and women alike. Inside, a similar canopy hovers over the space, outfitted with a corrugated metal bar, tile floor, wooden bar stools, chairs and tables adorned with classic Bacardi advertisements, where the Bacardi bat can soar.

BAR Architects

1660 Bush Street
San Francisco, CA 94109
415.441.4771
415.536.2323 (Fax)
www.bararch.com

BAR Architects

BAR Architects

Seven Restaurant
San Jose, California

Call them superstitious, but identical twins and co-executive chefs Russel and Curtis Valdez, along with their partner Hugh Parker, have named their new 3,500 square foot 108-seat restaurant and lounge "7". After all the address is 745 The Alameda and the number is lucky. Happily, guests like to visit for both the acclaimed contemporary American cuisine and the casual yet stylish contemporary interior designed by BAR Architects. Designed to provide casual dining by day and a sophisticated lounge by night, the space is both airy and intimate. High ceilings and tall windows on both sides of the restaurant maximize natural light and views to create a casual atmosphere for daytime dining. High backed leather booths, obscure glass screens and curtains—which close off part of the dining area and kitchen—provide an intimate space at night. The slightly elevated bar and lounge area overlooks the dining room, while the sleek open kitchen, designed as an integral part of the restaurant serves as a "stage" for both the restaurant and the street. Obscure glass windows with a small square of clear glass allow the chefs to look outside and pedestrians to view the chefs at work. The space dramatically celebrates such earthy materials as smooth concrete floors and walls, Venetian plaster accent walls and a curving, intricately textured entry wall of brick, softened with warm fabrics and comfortable furniture, enabling "7's" clientele to enjoy its simple yet elegant cuisine.

Top: Club booth with glass screen.

Left: Dining room.

Above: Open kitchen.

Opposite: Elliptical entry area.

Photography: Douglas Dun/Bar Architects, Tim Street-Porter.

BAR Architects

Sharon Heights Golf and Country Club
Menlo Park, California

Left: Exterior of new clubhouse.

Right: Main dining room.

Lower left: The Golf Lounge.

Lower right: New clubhouse from the 18th green.

Photography: Douglas Dun/ BAR Architects.

Approaching its 40th year of operations, the Sharon Heights Golf & Country Club recognized a shift in demographics required a larger facility that would serve the multi-faceted needs of its members; golfers and non-golfers alike. The solution involved replacing an older, small clubhouse with a new 50,000 square foot, two-story structure, which offers multiple uses and support venues to its varied membership. Designed by BAR Architects the new club provides an assortment of dining and banquet spaces accommodating events for up to 320 people, along with a pro-shop, lockers, fitness rooms and competition sized pool; all designed to serve a wider range of membership uses without impacting the golfing experience. Sited to fit an extremely narrow site and to capitalize on views to the golf course, the award-winning clubhouse maximizes views to the course and provides a spectacular panoramic backdrop for golfers finishing their play. The floor plan enables all of the public spaces to have ample access to natural light, gardens and the numerous outdoor terraces. The new design references the Shingle style of the original Sharon Mansion, the club's namesake, while contemporizing the detailing and color palette to preserve the warmth and inviting residential character that even this progressive organization still cherishes.

BAR Architects

Sundance Institute for the Arts
Sundance, Utah

The Sundance Institute for the Arts was founded in Sundance, Utah, by actor Robert Redford, to enhance the artistic vitality of American film as well as to nurture developing artists in a variety of disciplines. The Institute's diversity of interests is amply displayed and supported by the variety of buildings designed by BAR Architects. In addition to the 4,000 acre master plan for Sundance, BAR Architects designed the Rehearsal Pavilion where spaces can be divided or combined for dance, script readings, video taping and gatherings; a Screening Room that can accommodate lectures and concerts; a Village Center integrating new and renovated facilities including The General Store, Tree Room Restaurant, The Foundry Grill Restaurant—which includes three private dining rooms—The Owl Bar, the Sundance Deli and residential cottages. The Mandan Cottages (50 high quality condominiums) and The Pines (25 ski-in cottages) provide guest services for the Institute's participants and residents. The structure's unobtrusive physical presence, sensitivity to site conditions, respect for the environment and local construction practices serve to reinforce Sundance's basic values and provide facilities that support the arts and the artists.

Above left: Sundance Pines Lodge.

Below left: The Foundry Grill

Above: Exterior of the Screening Room.

Right: The Screening Room's interior with sliding doors.

Photography: Douglas Dun/BAR Architects, Andrew Kramer.

BAR Architects

Robert Mondavi Winery, To Kalon
Oakville, California

Left: Cellar Space.
Lower left: Tasting room.
Lower right: Retail Space
Photography: Douglas Dun/BAR Architects.

The challenge of creating an existing winery into an engaging complex that seamlessly integrates a visitor tour experience and expanded winery production space was successfully achieved by BAR Architects in their expansion and renovation of the Robert Mondavi Winery, To Kalon. Located in Oakville, California, BAR's design incorporates a new 76,000 square foot addition featuring gravity flow techniques, a 26,000 square foot renovation of the existing winery to produce high-end red wines and a redesigned winery tour sequence that follows the grapes from the vineyards through fermentation, aging and bottling, to the tasting room. Consulting with winery exhibit designer West Office Exhibition Design, BAR Architects also enhanced the reception, tasting and retail facilities; treating Cliff May's Mission-style building like the treasure vintage that it is.

Daroff Design Inc + DDI Architects, PC

2121 Market Street
Philadelphia
Pennsylvania 19103
215.636.9900
215.636.9627 (Fax)
info@daroffdesign.com
www.daroffdesign.com

Daroff Design Inc + DDI Architects, PC

Daroff Design Inc + DDI Architects, PC

Royal Pacific Resort
Universal Studios
Orlando, Florida

Right: Lobby reception.
Below: Orchid Court Lounge.
Opposite: Registration.
Photography: Peter Paige.

Reality goes on vacation in Orlando and Las Vegas, America's epicenters of fantasy entertainment, where nothing is quite what it seems and ordinary aspects of everyday life can become items of wonder. Even so, guests in Orlando's new, four-star, family-oriented Royal Pacific Resort, a Loews Hotel, at Universal Studios are registering surprise and delight over the architecture by Fugleberg Koch Architects and interior design by Daroff Design, which evoke a traditional Balinese village as it might have appeared in the 1930s. Set in an exuberant landscape of palm trees, exotic plants, bamboo forest and tropical lotus lagoon, the Royal Pacific immerses guests in an environment that compares favorably with the theme parks they come to visit, including Walt Disney World and Sea World as well as Universal Studios. What makes the Resort's

interior design particularly appealing is its blend of artistic invention and modern effectiveness, a combination maintained throughout such extensive facilities as the lobby, four restaurants, various bars and lounges, activity center with day care, arcade, fitness center, and 142,000-square foot meeting and convention center, along with 1,000 guestrooms and suites. Everywhere guests look, pause and touch within the three seven-story Guestroom Towers and two low-rise structures, the Reception and Function Buildings, is designed and furnished to transport them to another time and place without surrendering the conveniences of modern living. For a vacationing Indiana Jones and his family, this provides a wealth of memories, ranging from the telephone on the handsome teak wood night stand, equipped with its own data port, to Emeril Lagasse's new Tchoup Chop Restaurant, graced with its own waterfall.

Left: Orchid Court Lounge.
Right: Jake's American Bar.
Below: Jake's American Bar.
Opposite bottom: Bula Bar and Grill.

Daroff Design Inc + DDI Architects, PC

J.W. Marriott Hotel Miami
Miami, Florida

Above: Entrance to Lobby Bar.
Left: Lounge facing entry lobby.
Below left: Entry lobby.
Opposite: Lobby Bar.
Photography: Mary Nichols.

What a difference half a century has meant to prestigious Brickell Avenue in Miami, Florida. Where once millionaires' mansions lined the thoroughfare, the rise of the city as a center for Latin American and Caribbean finance in the 1970s and 1980s has created the largest concentration of international banking concerns in the nation. The recent opening of the 296-room, 22-story J.W. Marriott Hotel Miami, featuring an interior design by Daroff Design, marks the latest chapter in the narrative by bringing deluxe executive accommodations to the city's financial district, just two miles south of downtown. Traditional design and furnishings give an appropriate polish to such facilities as a concierge floor, bar and restaurant, business center, meeting and banquet space, spa, fitness center and outdoor pool to welcome visiting South American business travelers. The drama begins at the entry lobby, where an 18-foot high ceiling, marble staircase, bronze handrails and Makore wood paneling usher guests into the main lobby. Elsewhere, the aura of the Old World graces the New World. In such spaces as the Lobby Bar, paneling, coffered ceilings, and parquet floors, all in wood, with

46

plush carpet, beveled glass and leather-upholstered furniture combine to recreate a classic British club bar. Isabella's, a contemporary, 130-seat Spanish-themed restaurant features a covered dining terrace overlooking Brickell Avenue. The Trapiche Room is a specialty dining room where wines from the owner's Argentine vineyard are displayed on the walls. When the next pages in Miami's history are chronicled, they could very well be written here.

Top: Trapiche Room.

Above: Suite on concierge floor.

Right: Grand ballroom.

Di Leonardo International, Inc.

World Headquarters:
2350 Post Road
Suite 1
Warwick, Rhode Island 02886.2242
USA
401.732.2900
401.732.5315 (Fax)
info@dileonardo.com
www.dileonardo.com

Hong Kong
852.2.851.7282
852.2.851.7287 (Fax)

Offices:
Austin
Beijing
Dubai
Hong Kong

Di Leonardo International, Inc.

The Rosewood Hotel at the Al Faisaliah Center
Riyadh, Saudi Arabia

Even in Riyadh, Saudi Arabia's capital since 1932 and a showcase of modern architecture since the 1970s, the recently completed Al Faisaliah Center stands out. This mixed-use project, a five-star hotel, convention center, office tower, apartment building and shopping mall, was designed by Sir Norman Foster for the King Faisal Foundation, a leading philanthropic organization supporting numerous economic, academic and scientific programs. To create a 240,000-square foot hotel where world leaders and local businessmen could gather for business and pleasure, the King Faisal Foundation retained designer DiLeonardo International to produce a modern environment of restaurants, meeting rooms, lounges, banquet facility and spa as well as guest rooms that have won awards for quiet sophistication. Commenting about the interiors, H.R.H. Prince Bandar bin Saud bin Khaled, deputy managing director, praises DiLeonardo for its "exceptional contribution."

Above left: Transitional-style lounge.

Above right: Elevator lobby.

Top right: Restaurant.

Left: Lobby Lounge.

Opposite: Gourmet seafood restaurant.

Photography: Mike Wilson.

Di Leonardo MKV International, Ltd.

Grand Resort Lagonissi
Athens, Greece

With distant cultures crossing paths daily over land, sea, sky and Internet, creating a Polynesian and Japanese restaurant in a Mediterranean environment for a Greek hotel need not be a fantasy. In fact, DiLeonardo MKV recently designed Kohylia Restaurant & Sushi Bar, a 770-square meter (8,290-square foot) facility, for the Grand Resort Lagonissi, just minutes from the center of downtown Athens, by combining the freedom of Greek culture with the spirituality of Polynesia, accenting a palette of bamboo, stucco, stone and wood furniture with wondrous works of art. The hotel's guestrooms, by contrast, blend casual comfort with modern sophistication to produce a setting that opens itself to the surrounding environs. Either way, the Grand Resort is a stay worth seeing.

Above left: Stair to the restaurant.

Above right: Restaurant entry lobby.

Below left: Guest bath.

Below right: Guest suite.

Opposite: Restaurant bar.

Photography: Uxio de Vila Martinez.

Di Leonardo International, Inc.

Nashville Marriott at Vanderbilt University
Nashville, Tennessee

Who can resist Alma mater when she offers one or more memorable gathering places to attract students and faculty year-round, and welcome alumni to reunions and homecomings? For this reason, the all-new Nashville Marriott at Vanderbilt University, a 300,000-square foot, 11-story, 307-room facility designed by DiLeonardo International, has special significance for school and community alike. Its superb facilities, which include a restaurant, ballroom, meeting rooms, boardroom, hospitality suite and a stadium club adjoining the football stadium, reflect meetings with school representatives, extensive research on school culture, and diligent planning and design. Every detail evokes a sense of place unique to Vanderbilt—right down to the Gothic rails topped by contemporary newel posts.

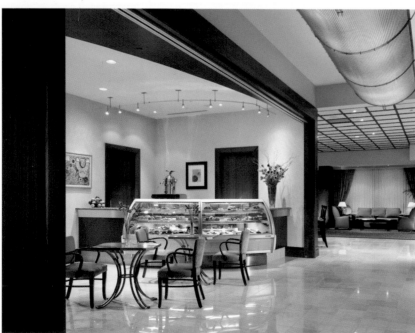

Upper left: Bar lounge.
Left: Cafe.

Above: Reception lobby.

Opposite lower left: Stair to ballroom.

Opposite lower right: Elevator lobby.

Photography: Gabriel Benzur.

Di Leonardo International, Inc.

Dumont Plaza
New York, New York

For the traveler who finds the typical hotel room a far cry from a home away from home or a satellite office, the 245 guestrooms and suites at the Dumont Plaza, on East 34th Street in midtown Manhattan, will represent an oasis of comfort and convenience. The rooms have been designed by DiLeonardo International as New York City apartments, complete with oversized furniture upholstered in wool and silk, European wardrobes, plush carpet, baseboards and ceiling moldings that match the Maccasar ebony casegoods, desks with power packs and computer ports, and ergonomic chairs for executives. Indeed, the traveler may insist on staying nowhere else.

Above: Work space with three-part desk unit.

Photography: Warren Jagger.

Below left: Full-length mirror and matching millwork.

Below center: Seating group overlooking Manhattan.

Below right: Bedroom and sitting area.

Dougall Design Associates, Inc.

35 North Arroyo Parkway
Suite 200
Pasadena, CA 91103
626.432.6464
626.432.6460 (Fax)
www.dougalldesign.com

Dougall Design Associates, Inc.

Borgata Hotel, Casino & Spa
Atlanic City, New Jersey

Thirteen years is a long wait in a society addicted to instant messaging, microwave ovens and 15-second commercials. However, that's how long Atlantic City has anticipated the opening of its latest, all-new casino. Judging from the rave reviews in the media and the crowds at the porte cochere, the Borgata Hotel Casino & Spa has been well worth the wait. This 2,002-room establishment, boasting such major public areas, designed by Dougall Design Associates, as the reception lobby, casino, restaurants, theater, event spaces, retail court and corridors, is not modest in its ambitions. Joint venture partners Boyd Gaming Corporation and MGM Mirage positioned the $1.1 billion-plus project to attract a younger and more sophisticated crowd than Atlantic City normally hosts. Sure enough, raising the standards in design, service and amenity to Las Vegas levels has not only made the competition pay attention, it has attracted a desirable clientele to a uncharted venue named Renaissance Pointe, a lush and newly forested site away from Atlantic City's fabled Boardwalk. But the parade of superlatives, including the 135,000-square foot casino, 10 specialty

Photography: Douglas Kahn, this page; J. Curtis, facing page. Above: Reception lobby with waterfall and programmed lighting.

Above: The Registaration Lobby

Left: Entrance to Amphora Lounge.

Opposite: Casino entrance flanked by Dale Chihuly sculpture.

Photography: Scott Frances Photography, New York

Above: The casino main entrance glass sculptures by Dale Chihuly.

Right: The VIP Tesoro Lounge.

Below right: A pause for refreshment in Gypsy Bar.

Opposite: B Bar main casino lounge.

boutiques, 11 restaurants, 50,000-square foot European spa, salon and barber shop, 70,000-square foot event center, 1,000-seat theater and 5,000-car guest parking garage, tells only part of the story. Dougall Design's vision for the Borgata is as Italian as its name, but its clean, contemporary yet luxurious environment chiefly evokes the excitement of modern, fashion-conscious Milan with only occasional references to the Renaissance and Baroque worlds of Florence and Rome. Highlights of the interiors by Dougall Design

Left: The Music Box theater that seats 1,000.

Below: Lighting defines Suilan.

Opposite upper left: Entrance to the Event Center.

Opposite lower right: Entrance to Suilan.

include the reception lobby, backed by a spectacular waterfall and programmed lighting, the casino, a majestic, vaulted hall bridging the 21st century and the Quattrocento, the Music Box theater, a 1,000-seat entertainment showcase styled like a 1940s jazz and supper club, and the retail piazza, a salute to Tuscan architecture with a pentagonal ceiling cupola and classic arcade. Among the numerous, unforgettable restaurants from Dougall Design are Specchio, named for chef Luke Palladino's antique handheld mirrors in glass cases lining the entranceway, Old Homestead Steakhouse, a bright, open space beneath a dramatic central rotunda soaring 23 feet to an oval ceiling,

Above: Speccio restaurant

Below left: Old Homestead Steakhouse.

Below Right: Entrance to Old Homestead Steakhouse Restaurant.

Suilan by Susanna Foo, honoring modern Asian design with a dining room dominated by a dark mahogany communal table and a display kitchen, and MIXX, a two-story restaurant and nightclub containing two bars, two lounges, and five private rooms with intertwined Asian and Latin themes. Like a roll of the dice, the odds have swiftly changed in Atlantic City, and the name of the game is the Borgata.

Earl Swensson Associates, Inc.

2100 West End Avenue
Suite 1200
Nashville TN 37203
615.329.9445
615.329.0046 (Fax)
www.esarch.com
info@esarch.com

Earl Swensson Associates, Inc.

Malliouhana Spa
Meads Bay
Anguilla, British West Indies

Affluent guests have repeatedly sought out a shimmering, white, Mediterranean-style hotel of 55 rooms and suites atop a panoramic bluff overlooking the blue waters of the Caribbean and the soft white sands of the beach, the Malliouhana on Meads Bay, Anguilla, British West Indies, since its founding by the Roydon family in 1982. Recently, the Hotel added a 15,000-square foot, two-level Spa, designed by Earl Swensson Associates and spa consultant Health Fitness Dynamics, that guests promptly claimed as their own. The Spa's appeal comes from its beautifully arranged and appointed facilities, which take their place within an elegant modern structure where indoor and outdoor spaces commingle. Whether guests are enjoying the a la carte treatment rooms, salon, boutique, fitness center or locker rooms on the first level or the private day suites on the second level, the Spa gives them yet another delectable reason to return.

Above left: Exterior elevation.

Above right: Treatment room.

Right: View to whirlpool and Meads Bay.

Below right: Outdoor shower.

Opposite: Private day suite.

Photography: Doug Scaletta.

Earl Swensson Associates, Inc. Boomtown Casino®
Bossier City, Louisiana

Above left: Arbor-covered entrance to Cattleman's Buffet.

Above right: Porte-cochere.

Right: Dessert display cases at Cattleman's Buffet.

Opposite: Sundance Cantina'ssm circular bar.

Photography: Scott McDonald/ Hedrich-Blessing.

How did Bossier City, Louisiana acquire a delightful Southwestern village that's drawing crowds to Pinnacle Entertainment'ssm Boomtown Casino? A recent renovation and expansion, designed by Earl Swensson Associates, updates the stationary boat casino with a charming ensemble of rustic, Southwestern-style structures, encompassing 39,738 square feet of renovated space and 538 square feet of new space. The existing pavilion has received a facelift and four new dining venues, including the Boomer's Cafesm, Cattleman's Buffet, Circle B Ranch Southwestern Bistrosm and Sundance Cantinasm, add a

seemingly timeless ambiance born of stucco-like wall coatings, Mexican tiles, carved wood, wrought iron and more. Timeless or not, guests love it. As Cliff Kortman, senior vice president, construction and development of Pinnacle reports, "Our business increased over 300 percent year over year."

Earl Swensson Associates, Inc.

The Spa at The Hotel Hershey
Hershey, Pennsylvania

Imagine yourself relaxing in a Whipped Cocoa Bath or indulging in a Chocolate Fondue Wrap. These healthy confections are just part of the allure at The Spa at The Hotel Hershey, a newly completed, 17,000-square-foot, three-story European-style spa, designed by Earl Swensson Associates with TAG Galyean, which evokes historic High Point, the estate home of chocolate magnate Milton Hershey and his wife Catherine. The Spa augments the Mediterranean-style, 234-room, landmark Hotel Hershey, built in 1933 on 300 acres overlooking the beloved "Chocolate Town." Its design reflects the need for a seamless addition to the existing architecture, and the unique, high-end features expected of world-class spas. Here guests happily succumb to eight massage rooms, five facial rooms, four wet treatment rooms, four soaking tubs, two signature showers, two steam rooms, inhalation room, two hair-styling salons and more in an elegant, residential environment of stained glass windows, hardwood floors, pecan paneling, arched Palladian windows and a sky-painted dome ceiling that offers the perfect setting for such pleasures as a Strawberry Parfait Scrub.

Above left: 'Quiet room' with fireplace.

Above right: Spa exterior.

Right: Reception with retail display.

Far right: Treatment room.

Opposite: Women's vanity area.

Photography: Craig Dugan/ Hedrich-Blessing.

Earl Swensson Associates, Inc.

Hilton Suites Dallas North
Dallas, Texas

Above left: Fountain lobby.
Above right: Porte cochere.
Left: Billiards lounge.
Photography: Doug Scaletta.

Business travelers facing more than one- or two-night stays appreciate the new Hilton Suites Dallas North. Located in an upscale area of Dallas near the popular Galleria shopping center, the 204,774-square foot, 12-story, 258-room facility, designed by Earl Swensson Associates, combines the residential accommodations of suites with the amenities and comforts of a full service hotel. Each suite, for example, offers a living/lounge space, bedroom, refrigerator, microwave and coffee maker, as well as high-speed Internet service. Such features as a fountain lobby, 3,025 square feet of meeting space, boardroom, business center, billiards lounge area, bar, gift shop, indoor pool and exercise room complete this vision of working and living in a gracious Texas interior of mahogany, cherry, terra cotta and beige.

Elness Swenson Graham Architects Inc.

700 Third Street South
Minneapolis
Minnesota 55415
612.339.5508
612.339.5382 (Fax)
www.esgarch.com

Elness Swenson Graham Architects Inc.

Elness Swenson Graham Architects Inc.

Milwaukee Road Depot
Minneapolis, Minnesota

Left: Historic head house and new hotel porte-cochere.

Below: Hotel lounge.

Opposite: Banquet facility in head house.

Photography: Dana Wheelock.

Although the last train pulled out of Minneapolis's Milwaukee Road Depot in 1971, try explaining this to the children playing in the water park at the former railroad terminus. A locomotive is part of the water park's highly animated "train slide" that builds to a climax of spraying water, light and train sounds at regular intervals, and one of many reasons why the 1899 Depot is contributing to the life of Minneapolis once more. After three decades of attempted redevelopment, the landmark has been transformed by CSM Corporation, the City of Minneapolis, Elness Swenson Graham Architects and Shea Inc. into a handsome, multi-use facility that incorporates the original train station in a larger scheme including badly needed downtown hotels, public indoor ice rink, video arcade, snack bar and parking for 666 cars, along with the water park. The key to the award-winning design

has been the adaptation of the existing architecture to compatible new uses, and the addition of new structures to complement the historic site without overshadowing it. The historic Depot, for example, brings vitality to the shed with the ice rink and at-grade parking, while the head house converts its large interior expanses into a banquet facility at street level and 21 custom hotel suites upstairs. New construction, which comprises a 204-room, five-story Marriott Courtyard Hotel attached to the head house, the water park, and a four-story, 130-room Residence Inn Hotel, enables the Depot to encircle its city block, restoring a much appreciated sense of wholeness to downtown Minneapolis—with or without the trains.

Top: Living room in hotel suite.

Above: Water park linking the hotels.

Right: Bedroom.

Above: View showing adaptation of existing architecture to new structures.

Left: Historic shed housing ice rink.

Elness Swenson Graham Architects Inc.

Radisson Hotel at Carlson Park
San Antonio, Texas

Above: Radisson Hotel.

Above right: Chazz restaurant.

Right: Outdoor dining area.

Opposite: Patio.

Photography: Greer & Associates.

Baby boomers have served notice that their retirement years will be as active as their careers, inspiring such attractive new housing and hospitality options as the Radisson Hotel at Carlson Park, designed by Elness Swenson Graham Architects, in San Antonio's beautiful Hill Country. The 172,500-square foot project, which caters to affluent empty nesters, is seen as a proto-type by its developers, innkeeper Carlson Hospitality Worldwide and design/build developer Ryan Companies. Consequently, the 227-key resort hotel shares its 27-acre site with 108 condominiums in four four-story buildings and 72 town houses, adjacent to the Arthur Hill-designed Hill Country Golf Course. The hotel is outstanding in its own right, featuring 50 suites with large balconies, meeting rooms, specialty restaurant (Chazz, designed by Arnold Syrop Associates),

bar and lounge, swimming pools and signature spa, all constructed in the Hill Country vernacular. Exteriors make generous use of native Texas limestone and metal roofs, while interiors evoke Texas ranches with dark wood beams, stone fireplaces and comfortable, traditional-style furnishings. The Carlson Park Club provides dining, recreational facilities and other services from the hotel. Their community beyond the hotel has amenities of its own, to be sure, such as four swimming pools, library, 30-seat theater and a country club-style dining room It seems safe to say that baby boomers will enthusiastically embrace this concept.

Above: Town house.

Below left: Bar.

Below right: Fireplace lounge.

Engstrom Design Group / edg

1201 Fifth Avenue
San Rafael, CA 94901
415.454.2277
415.454.2278 (Fax)
www.engstromdesign.com

Engstrom Design Group / edg

Engstrom Design Group / edg

Brasserie Vert
Hollywood & Highland Center
Hollywood, California

Hooray for Hollywood! Brasserie Vert, developed by the Wolfgang Puck Fine Dining Group at the Hollywood & Highland Center, is a new, 167-seat casual restaurant and bar that's building traffic at the shopping and entertainment complex recently created to revive the city's heart. As designed by Engstrom Design Group, Vert represents a lively interpretation of a French bistro, whose soft plaster walls, ceilings of aged barn beams and mottled concrete floors draw attention to the large, communal bar. Every detail is modeled, including the custom lighting fixtures, sofa-like booths, floating islands of modern furniture, open, stainless steel kitchen and a high-style mirror with the daily menu written in grease pencil, to give working or would-be stars and moguls a perfect scene for such brasserie/trattoria entrees from executive chef Lee Hefter and chef Matt Bencivenga as Grilled Tuna with Cannelini Beans, Veal New York Steak "au Poivre" or Sizzling Mussels Mueniere.

Engstrom Design Group / edg

Jasper's
Legacy Center
Plano, Texas

"Just like a backyard cookout should be. Without the mosquitoes," is how the Dallas Morning News recently described Jasper's, the new, 235-seat, "New Texas Cuisine" restaurant, designed by Engstrom Design Group, at the Legacy Center in Plano, Texas. Indeed, the restaurant's contemporary take on a casual indoor/outdoor space, combining teak outdoor style chairs, benches and tables with artistic interpretations of the Texas landscape under dark ceilings with large, custom lighting fixtures, is playing to raves in metropolitan "Big D." Guests seated in the bar/lounge, semi-private dining area with picnic-style furniture, board room with frosted glass or 50-seat private room can admire the symbolic landscape of low, woven-wood open dividers, bronze mesh screens and sculptural steel rods while waiting for their orders to arrive. Then they can enjoy executive chef Kent Rathbun's solid fare, featuring barbecue ribs, various steaks, a "miraculous version" of macaroni and cheese, and mini malted-milk shakes "to die for," confident the rugged green tabletops can hold it all—they're made of solid concrete.

Above: View of main dining area.

Left: Bronze mesh screens as space dividers.

Right: Bar/lounge.

Opposite: Dining area with fireplace and steel rods as prairie grass.

Photography: Richard Klein.

Given Hawaii's beautiful Wailea Beach on Maui as a backdrop, the Four Seasons Resort Maui has been offering hospitality of such unstinting luxury, flawless service, abundant recreational activities and sumptuous accommodations that even seasoned travelers lavish praise on it. Naturally, expectations for the hotel's new, 200-seat Spago restaurant, designed for the Wolfgang Puck Fine Dining Group by Engstrom Design Group, have been high. Spago would replace an underutlized, all-day hotel restaurant with an elegant yet family-friendly destination restaurant created by celebrated chef Wolfgang Puck to offer such fresh, Asian-French dishes as Pan-Roasted Opakapaka, Roasted Duck with Pineapple and Grilled Cote De Boeuf. Happily, the rebirth of the 8,700-square foot space has been a complete success,

opening up the rooms with ocean views, installing a bar, lounge dining and outdoor seating under a covered lanai, and incorporating rich materials, saturated colors, panoramic photomurals and opulent fabrics. Now, Four Seasons guests are not the only diners waiting for tables at Spago—the sincerest compliment a restaurant hotel can receive.

Left: Main dining room.

Top: A distinctive soffit evokes ocean waves.

Above right: Outdoor seating under a lanai.

Right: Photomural installation behind back bar.

Photography: Cesar Rubio.

Engstrom Design Group / edg

Wolfgang Puck Express Prototype
Cool Springs Center
Nashville, Tennessee

Left: Counter seating with cooking behind.

Above: Dining room.

Below: Pick-up/take-out stations.

Photography: Larry Falke.

How do you bring the youthful and lively southern California attitude associated with master chef Wolfgang Puck to a 4,400-square foot, 134-seat fast-casual restaurant in a suburban Nashville shopping mall? The challenge for Ted Moats, who holds the Wolfgang Puck Express franchise for central Tennessee, Georgia and most of Florida, was to offer guests a cooking experience in true Puck fashion. Engstrom Design Group devised a prototype for Wolfgang Puck Worldwide that includes a compact, linear kitchen and dining room where guests could sit, dine and observe the preparations within a stylish, playful and comfortable interior of granite, cherry wood, tile and stainless steel that comes with Puck himself—via a plasma screen, at least.

Fugleberg Koch

2555 Temple Trail
Winter Park, FL 32789
800.393.0595
407.628.1057 (Fax)
www.fuglebergkoch.com

Fugleberg Koch

Fugleberg Koch

Royal Pacific Resort at
Universal Orlando, a Loews Hotel
Orlando, Florida

Imagine standing at the entryway to the South Pacific with your bags at your side and no need for a passport, visa, inoculations or other encumbrances of overseas travel. Welcome to the Royal Pacific Resort at Universal Orlando, A Loews Hotel, in Orlando, Florida. A land of swaying palm trees, a sandy beach, pathways lined with hand-carved stone lanterns, exotic flowers, a lush, bamboo forest and hand-carved stone elephants. As conceived by Fugleberg Koch Architects, this five-building, 1,000-room, 49-acre resort transports guests to a South Pacific Village in the 1930s, a time when guests boarded great "flying boats" to go island hopping as only the wealthy and privileged could do. Especially impressive about this complex, is that its efficient, comfortable and thoroughly enchanting environment was designed in

Above: Lagoon shoreline.

Lower left: Lagoon pool.

Lower right: Function building.

Opposite: Reception entry bridge at porte cochere.

Photography: Peter Paige and Larry Taylor.

Left: Reception building.
Below: Lobby bar and lounge.

just six months and completed on time and under budget. Comprising a three-level reception building, one-level function building, three seven-level guest towers, 5,000 square foot fitness center, 75,000 square foot meeting and event space, 12,000 square foot lagoon pool, three restaurants, bar/lounge, children's activity center, and Royal Garden with putting green and entertainment/stage area, guests are enthusiastically applauding the experience that begins the moment they cross a bamboo bridge from the porte cochere into an exotic world. Custom-made furniture, wood carvings and sculpture made by craftsmen in Bali are equally impressive.

Fugleberg Koch

Crowne Plaza Universal Hotel
Orlando, Florida

Left: Main entrance.
Below: Port cochere.
Opposite: Atrium.
Photography: Larry Taylor.

Guests may never realize that Orlando's striking, new, 15-story, 400-room Crowne Plaza Universal began as an incomplete 200-room condominium hotel atrium tower with in-place utilities and a restricted parking plan that sat dormant for several years on Universal Boulevard, just a short walk from the city's celebrated International Drive. But after Group One Productions, a sister company to Fugleberg Koch Architects, researched the building's potential, Crowne Plaza took control and engaged Fugleberg Koch Architects to create a new facility on the compact site. By attaching a double-loaded corridor tower to the existing atrium tower and adding public facilities such as dining and meeting spaces, the renovation has been a complete success. The existing tower accommodates part of a new, upgraded HVAC system,

with the balance being assigned to the new tower, and the two structures are joined as one by a unified facade treatment. Inside, an urbane, transitional interior blending the Park Avenue elegance of New York with the Art Deco chic of Miami's South Beach gives such facilities as the guest rooms, landscaped courtyard, 5,000-square foot banquet and meeting space, Arcanjo's bistro restaurant, Market Café, business center, pool and fitness center their suave appeal, combining brushed metal with polished soft woods and classic tile in tones of pink, lavender, gray and blue. Whether guests are heading to Universal Studios, Sea World or Walt Disney world, the Crowne Plaza Universal offers a most delightful way to begin a visit to central Florida.

Top: Rear view from pool deck.
Above left: Guest suite.
Above right: Arcanjo's Bistro.

Glen & Company

Glen Coben Architecture & Design, PLLC
13 East 37 Street
Suite 7A
New York, NY 10016
212.689.2779
212.689.1033 (Fax)
www.glenandcompany.com
glen@glenandcompany.com

Glen & Company Washington Park Restaurant
New York, New York

Though reminders of the flowering of American modernism in the 1920s and 1930s abound in the literature, music, art and cinema of the era, New Yorkers can just step outdoors to enjoy such icons of Art Deco architecture as William van Alen's Chrysler Building. Not surprisingly, the love affair between the city and its Art Deco heritage endures. For example, at the historic Fifth Avenue Hotel in Greenwich Village, designed by Emery Roth in 1929, the new

Washington Park Restaurant combines a restored Art Deco terrazzo floor and plaster ceiling with a contemporary interpretation of the style by Glen & Company to delight guests drawn to noted California chef Jonathan Waxman's modern American fare. The design of the 3,000-square foot, 120-seat restaurant frames the open kitchen of Italian and Portuguese tile within a proscenium arch as the focal point, and enriches the dining room with an onyx bar,

butter-colored plaster walls, cafe chairs from France and sensuous leather and mohair upholstered dining chairs to create the perfect setting for such culinary delights as red pepper pancakes with smoked salmon, caviar and creme fraiche.

Above: Open kitchen.

Opposite lower left: Dining room.

Photography: Ofer Wallberger.

Glen & Company Flatotel International
New York, New York

A cosmopolitan, intimate and affordable hotel in midtown Manhattan offering 460 crisply tailored one- and two-bedroom suites appointed in custom-designed contemporary furnishings and state-of-the-art amenities might sound more like a stage set for a Broadway musical by Cole Porter, George Gershwin or Richard Rodgers than an enticing reality. However, the 50-story Flatotel International, a conversion of a luxury apartment by Glen & Company, is anything but song and dance. In addition to a limestone bath and fully equipped gourmet kitchen, each suite comes equipped with such conveniences as cable TV, VCR, CD player, data port and high-speed Internet access. A fitness center, business center and Moda, the on-site restaurant designed by Glen & Company are also available to all guests, along with such legendary tourist attractions as the Museum of Modern Art, Rockefeller Center, Fifth Avenue's elite shops, Carnegie Hall and of course, Broadway's theaters, just a song and a dance away.

Top: Bathroom.

Above: Bed in wall-mounted position.

Left: Bed in freestanding position.

Below: Desk and office chair in room with freestanding bed.

Right: Lobby area.

Photography: Bruce Buck. Lobby photo by Paul Warchol.

Glen & Company

So many shoppers visit the retail stores introduced by some of their favorite mail order catalogues that QVC, the cable TV shopping service, has now opened its own at the Mall of America, in Bloomington, Minnesota, combining retailing, broadcasting and marketing. The 2,500-square foot QVC @ The Mall, designed by Glen & Company, is not your everyday store. For example, QVC transmits over 52 live broadcasts annually, hosted by on-air personalities, to some 77 million U.S. households from the store's broadcast facility. Inside a storefront that resembles an ordinary house, the interior looks as if it were being pulled apart, letting individual rooms showcase QVC products in appropriate environments. Will consumers embrace "a unique shopping experience allowing you to see, touch and purchase much of the same merchandise you can acquire through QVC's television program or through QVC.com?" Stay tuned, same store, same mall, same time, to find out.

Left: Foyer.
Above: Storefront.
Photography: Greg Page.

Glen & Company

WishList
Greenwich, Connecticut

Left: Fitting rooms.
Above: Cashwrap.
Below: Typical store fixtures.
Photography: Jim Lee.

Forget what you've heard about suburban stereotypes and Stepford wives. Take a good look at what hip teenage girls and their adventurous older sisters are wearing in storied, affluent Greenwich, Connecticut: belly-baring jeans, mini skirts and the shortest shorts, wearing labels such as Miss Sixty, Blue Cult, Diesel, Hudson, Juicy Couture and Michael Stars? WishList, a savvy retailer with a lucrative niche for fashion-forward apparel in nearby Westport, Connecticut, has now made the jump to a 2,000-square foot store in Greenwich, designed by Glen & Company. Like other effective selling spaces, WishList complements its merchandise without overpowering it. Yet the interior offers delights of its own, such as whimsical inspirational quotations on the walls, suave lounge furniture, a candy counter and fixtures that suggest how a hip, organized closet should really look. Where do Greenwich fashionistas go for graduation and prom dresses by Betsey Johnson, Shoshanna, Laundry and BCBG? Now you know.

Glen & Company

The Joy of Flight
Terminal One, Fort Lauderdale/
Hollywood International Airport
Fort Lauderdale, Florida

Only the bravest or hardiest airline passengers might celebrate the joy of flight amidst the heightened security that has enveloped airports after September 11, 2001. Yet the mastery of powered flight by the Wright Brothers on December 17, 1903 brought genuine happiness to humanity. The Joy of Flight, a 450-foot-long sculpture by Glen & Company at Fort Lauderdale/Hollywood International Airport's new Terminal One, expresses this achievement succinctly in 12 mobiles of perforated metal inspired by paper airplanes. Each mobile, with wingspans from 8-22 feet, is suspended from a serpentine truss, capturing sentiments we will revive someday.

Above: Serpentine truss and mobiles.
Right: Mobile.
Far right: Mobile.
Photography: Victor Colon.

Haverson Architecture and Design, PC

63 Church Street
Greenwich
Connecticut 06830
203.629.8300
203.629.8399 (Fax)
www.haversonarchitecture.com

Haverson Architecture and Design, PC

Haverson Architecture and Design, PC

Nyla
New York, New York

Above left: Grand staircase, bridge and bar.

Above right: Mezzanine seating.

Upper right: Entrance.

Opposite: Main dining room as seen from bridge.

Photography: Peter Paige Photography.

Opening a restaurant is a dream celebrities share with everyone else—except that individuals like singer Britney Spears can make the dream come true. Accordingly, Spears launched Nyla, a 7,000-square foot, 160-seat restaurant in midtown Manhattan, designed by Haverson Architecture and Design. Nyla, a name combining New York and Louisiana, Spears' home state, creatively transforms the space once built for the Chemist's Club to welcome guests for eclectic fare and people watching. The contemporary design focuses on a grand staircase joining the main floor to the mezzanine via a glass bridge in the Club's former social hall. Here, original mahogany paneling, plaster coffered ceiling and monumental fireplace contrast dramatically with a playful, 14-foot diameter chandelier, radiant bar areas and colorful textiles used extensively for curtains, wall hangings, column wraps and banquettes. For songbirds seeking a hamburger with handcut fries and chipotle mayonnaise, a duck and wild mushroom etouffee or crabcakes, Nyla provides many a fine perch.

Haverson Architecture and Design, PC

Restaurant rm
New York, New York

Seafood is the catch of the day at noted chef/owner Rick Moonen's new rm, a 3,000-square foot, 120-seat, two-story restaurant on New York's Upper East Side, designed by Haverson Architecture and Design. In an inspired adaptation of a townhouse that retains its previous restaurant layout to save time and cost, the new design establishes a warm, nautical flavor in the narrow, low-ceiling space without resorting to theatricality. In the main dining room, for example, arched beams span its width and establish an intimate scale, accentuated by a wood-ribbed, translucent soffit, steel cables and turnbuckles crossing the beams, banquettes sectioned into smaller areas, low walls detailed in mahogany and copper, and aquatic sculpture and photography. To complete the image, guests reel in such signature entrees as spice-seared Yellowtail "tataki," pan-roasted scallops with oxtail and tomato-mustard jam, or potato-wrapped baked Walleye in creamy leek-truffle-chanterelle froth.

Above: Main dining room.

Left: Wine display.

Upper left: Entrance.

Photography: Peter Paige Photography.

Haverson Architecture and Design, PC

Smith & Wollensky
Dallas, Texas

Who's afraid of aged steak or prime rib? Not Americans, who consume beef with singular passion when dining out. That's why Smith & Wollensky, one of the nation's most successful high-end steakhouses, recently opened its eighth location, in Dallas, Texas. The 11,000-square foot, 350-seat restaurant, designed by Haverson Architecture and Design, honors restaurateur Alan Stillman's instructions to "Make it look old!" by inviting guests into an environment that appears to predate its surroundings. Starting with a facade treatment that adds 100 years to its age, the design introduces hints of a place that has evolved over time in the entry where wine display meets a boisterous bar and elegant dining room. The rooms flow together in a quirky, eccentric way, and their building materials, furnishings and Americana collection—a trademark of Smith & Wollensky—preserve a bygone era that guests can revisit for hearty meals with superb wine.

Above: Main dining room.
Right: Entry view.
Upper right: Exterior.
Photography: Peter Paige Photography.

Haverson Architecture and Design, PC

¡Bamba!
Greenwich, Connecticut

Left: Fireplace in parlor dining room.

Below left: Bar.

Below right: Waterfall, stairway and remodeled plantation ceiling.

Photography: Peter Paige Photography.

Caribbean cuisine has arrived in the quintessential New England town of Greenwich, Connecticut, founded in 1646. In the stately, turn-of-the-century former residence of a prominent family, restaurateur Maggie Zakka has created 3,000-square foot, 100-seat ¡Bamba! to serve Nuevo-Latino cuisine. The design by Haverson Architecture and Design transforms the residence into a gracious Caribbean plantation home, so the central stairhall becomes the main dining room, the parlor is a smaller dining room, and the porch shelters a whimsical bar. While the makeover respects the former residence, relying on such brightly colored paint, paddle fans, multi-toned, beaded glass light fixtures, lattice and tropical plants, there's also a 1½ story indoor waterfall beside the staircase—a touch of Yankee ingenuity.

Haverson Architecture and Design, PC

Many who pass through New York's landmark Grand Central Station know about the award-winning cheesecakes "to die for" from Junior's, a Brooklyn restaurant run by the third generation of the Rosen family. Accordingly, the Rosen's have opened Junior's on the Station's lower concourse and Junior's Dessert Shop on the upper one, both designed by Haverson Architecture and Design. The 75-seat Cafe uses an ornamental iron gate and bridge-like ramp to enclose a space for cafe tables and chairs in front of former ticket windows. The Dessert Shop, by contrast, applies glass extensively to display its cheesecakes and other sweets in cherry hardwood cases behind a clear glass storefront. Historic Brooklyn photographs complete the design by functioning as environmental graphics and poignant reminders of the fun and food shared by this fabled borough and its city.

Top right: Junior's Cafe.

Far right: Junior's Dessert Shop.

Right: View from above.

Photography: Paul Warchol.

Haverson Architecture and Design, PC

Katzenberg's Express
Greenwich, Connecticut

Katzenberg's Express represents the early '60s short-order delicatessen/restaurant many communities wish they had saved—except that Greenwich, Connecticut just welcomed the new, 2,000-square foot, 50-seat space, designed by Haverson Architecture and Design. Photographs from the owner's family album are coupled with the decor to unabashedly revel in the trappings of a younger America. Guests will find such period details as curved lunch counters, ribbed, aluminum-edged Formica tabletops, boomerang-patterned upholstery, futuristically styled stools, uplighted, kidney-shaped ceiling planes and cantilevered shelves, served with such classics as frankfurters, homemade baked goods and "design your own sandwich" specialties. If this is deja-vu, nobody's complaining.

Left: Overall view.

Upper left: Counter dining.

Upper right: Seating and take-out counter.

Photography: Paul Warchol.

HBA / Hirsch Bedner Associates

3216 Nebraska Avenue
Santa Monica, California 90404
310.829.9087
310.453.1182 (Fax)
www.hbadesign.com

Atlanta
Dubai
Hong Kong
London
Los Angeles
New Delhi
San Francisco
Singapore

HBA / Hirsch Bedner Associates

The Fullerton Hotel
Singapore

Above left: Jade Restaurant entrance.

Above right:: The "Far East" suite.

Left: Master bedroom/study den.

Lower left: Private dining room at Jade.

Opposite: Atrium Courtyard Lounge.

Photography: Peter Mealin.

Often overshadowed by the skyscrapers built during Singapore's spectacular economic ascent are the splendid buildings of its British colonial era. However, the Fullerton Hotel won't be one of them. Designed by Keys & Dowdeswell and built in 1928 as a Neo-Palladian colonial post office, the building recently reopened as a luxurious, 400-room, 43,332-square meter hotel, transformed by HBA/Hirsch Bedner Associates. A panoramic, nine-story Atrium, housing the reception area, Atrium Courtyard Lounge, Town Restaurant, Post Bar and Jade Restaurant in a bamboo grove, forms the heart of the facility. Other key public areas, including the Straits

Club, the Lighthouse Restaurant on the top floor, column-free, 450-person column free Ballroom, Business Center and meeting/function rooms at the foot of the Grand Staircase, and an Asian-style Spa, add luster to the 100-plus room types. The acclaimed adaptation, overcoming a challenging footprint and combining traditional and contemporary design with a residential feel, makes the Fullerton a vibrant symbol of the "New Asia."

HBA / Hirsch Bedner Associates   St. Regis Shanghai
Shanghai, China

It's not easy impressing Shanghai, a city long accustomed to the world's rich and famous strolling its fabled Bund. Yet few residents would doubt that the St. Regis Shanghai, a new, 40-story, 318-room, five-star hotel, has become one of the city's prime people-watching places. Its interior design, by HBA/Hirsch Bedner Associates, draws inspiration from the world's great opera houses to exploit the drama in the high-rise structure. As a result, the triple-height lobby feels like a theater, the restaurants present superb cuisine and service in opulent surroundings, and guestrooms offer Old World luxury with high technology. In a city where nothing escapes notice, the opulent Imperial Suite on the top two floors impresses everyone.

Above: Lobby.

Left: "Danieli's" Restaurant.

Opposite upper left: Imperial Suite.

Opposite lower left: "Carianna" Chinese Restaurant.

Opposite lower right: Indoor swimming pool.

Photography: Jaime Ardiles-Arce.

HBA / Hirsch Bedner Associates

One & Only Le Touessrok Resort & Spa
Mauritius

Above: Lobby.
Below left: Bath.
Below right: Bedroom.
Photography: Chris Tubbs.

Jetsetters eager for the next chic getaway have a new temptation, thanks to an impressive remodeling of Le Touessrok Resort & Spa, a 200-room hotel on the island of Mauritius, 500 miles east of Madagascar in the Indian Ocean. The comprehensive facelift by HBA/Hirsch Bedner Associates launches the new, deluxe One & Only hotels for noted hotelier Sol Kerzner. Kerzner sought to accentuate the existing, village-like ambiance, create more spacious guestrooms, and introduce a distinctive style to reflect the exotic location. Consequently, Le Touessrok is quite unlike its rivals, a formidable achievement in a market with nearly 100 hotels. Revered as the island's "grand dame," Le Touessrok breaks with the prevailing colonial style among luxury hotels by embracing colors derived from island flowers, artwork and wall mosaics inspired by Indian culture (Indians arrived en masse during the British era) and fresh design concepts, such as open bathrooms boasting freestanding, egg-shaped bathtubs with direct views of the Indian Ocean. Has the makeover paid off? Let the wealthy young Europeans lining up at the poolside bar reply.

Above: "Barlen's" Restaurant.

Right: Spa.

119

HBA / Hirsch Bedner Associates

Hotel Grand Bretagne
Athens, Greece

History doesn't repeat itself, but Belle Époque-era guests of the Grande Bretagne Hotel, a wealthy expatriate Greek's former Athens residence converted into a grand hotel in 1872, could surely find their way through the newly finished restoration by HBA/Hirsch Bedner Associates. The intent for the 323-room (including 60 suites) Grand Bretagne, traditionally the domain of royal families, celebrities and artists, was to regain its original character after years of alteration. Working with archival photographs and drawings, the designers developed a sumptuous new "historic interior" complete with the latest in services and amenities. The reconstruction has proceeded with such attention to detail and concern for guests' needs that visitors can hardly believe the space—lobby, Winter Garden, bar, restaurants, ballrooms, spa, guestrooms and suites—materialized only after the building was gutted. Indeed, just steps from the business district, fashionable Kolonaki Square and the picturesque old quarter of Plaka, history has nearly repeated itself.

Above: "GB Corner" Restaurant.
Below left: "Alexander's" Bar.
Below right: Bedroom in suite.
Bottom right: Lobby.
Photography:
Jaime Ardiles-Arce.

Hill Glazier Architects

925 Alma Street
Palo Alto, CA 94301
650.617.0366
650.617.0373 (Fax)
www.hillglazier.com

Hill Glazier Architects

Hill Glazier Architects

Left: Reception and lobby.

Above left: View off the balcony overlooking the Pacific Ocean.

Above right: Main entrance and porte cochere.

Photography: Clayton James.

Legions of artists and actors, attracted to the lush Laguna Beach landscape of white sand beaches, quiet coves and rolling hills since the early 1900s, have not spoiled the southern California community that the Spaniards named Canada de las Lagunas or "Canyon of the Lakes." An example of how this idyllic environment renews itself is the Montage Resort & Spa, a new, 211-room, 21-suite hotel designed by Hill Glazier Architects. Perched on a coastal bluff, the Montage protects neighbors' views by positioning itself below the view plane of the Pacific Coast hillside and de-emphasizing the scale of its hotel, 37 beach bungaloes and parking garage. Yet its careful siting ensures that all of its guestrooms and most of its public spaces enjoy spectacular views both indoors and out, the lobby, lounge, two restaurants, bar and grill, spa and guestrooms honor the Golden State's Craftsman tradition with their interior architecture of wood and stone, burnishing the appeal of a place that stars such as Bette Davis, Charlie Chaplin, Mary Pickford, Rudolph Valentino, Judy Garland and Mickey Rooney have called home.

Hill Glazier Architects

Hyatt Regency Tamaya Resort & Spa
Santa Ana Pueblo, New Mexico

Below left: Lobby lounge.

Below right: Golf course and hotel buildings.

Bottom left: A view towards Sandia Peak and the surrounding mountains.

Photography: Mark Knight

A world apart from New Mexico's metropolises of Albuquerque and Santa Fe, tourist attractions in Taos, and nuclear laboratories at Los Alamos is the Pueblo of Santa Ana, a Native American tribal community where the Tamayame live on a sunny, semi-arid yet handsome reservation. To welcome vacationers to the area, the Pueblo recently built the 360,000-square foot, 350-room Hyatt Regency Tamaya Resort & Spa, designed by Hill Glazier Architects, on tribal land adjacent to the Rio Grande with views of scenic Sandia Peak. The design's interconnecting grids convey an organic feel that suggests its construction lasted several centuries, much like the pueblos. And when guests are not busy enjoying the restaurant, cafe, two bars, delicatessen, lounge, outdoor swimming pool, 13,500-square foot spa and 18-hole golf course, they can explore Pueblo culture in an adjacent tribal museum—or the world outside their hotel.

Hill Glazier Architects

Four Seasons Sharm El Sheikh
Sinai Peninsula, Egypt

A flurry of hotel development in the last decade at Sharm El Sheikh, an Egyptian resort defined by the Sinai Desert at its back and the uncannily clear waters of the Red Sea off its shores, has not diminished the debut of the Four Seasons Sharm El Sheikh, a 136-room hotel designed by Hill Glazier Architects. Rising from a hillside like a lush oasis whose buildings, gardens and palm trees define a traditional-looking, village-like cluster of one- and two-story guest accommodations, the Four Seasons is quite unlike other local hotels. The product of a study of traditional Arabic architecture as well as a response to world travelers' needs, the Four Seasons offers its two lounges, two restaurants, ballroom, spa, pools, tennis courts and boutique shopping in a charming, vernacular setting. And since this hotel is at Sharm El Sheikh, it also offers world-class coral reef snorkeling and scuba diving, right off its own jetty.

Above: Lounge.

Left: Waha Poolside Bar and Restaurant.

Below: Outdoor courtyard.

Opposite: Exterior vista.

Photography: Peter Vitale, John Warburton-Lee.

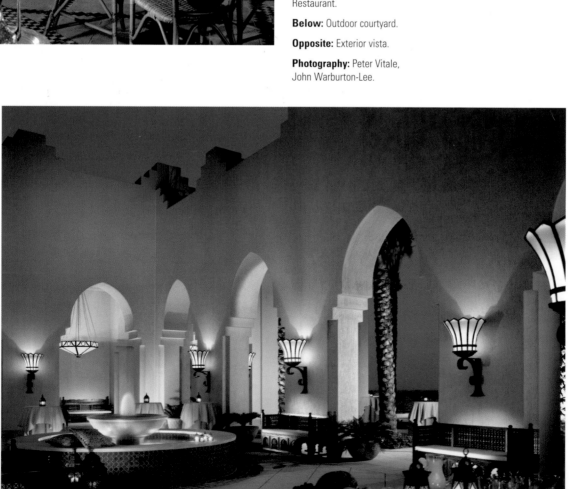

Hill Glazier Architects

The Ritz Carlton Bachelor Gulch
Vail, Colorado

Think of a luxury ski resort with 237 guestrooms and 52 club units that resembles a private residence. That's how Hill Glazier Architects was instructed to design the new Ritz Carlton Bachelor Gulch, in Vail, Colorado. Designed in the tradition of the grand National Park lodges of the west, appreciative guests keep the hotel's lobby lounge, library, restaurant, bar, 21,000-square foot spa, children's activity center, meeting rooms and ballroom lively and full—at least when they're not heading for the ski-in/ski-out facilities, 36 holes of golf, hiking, fly fishing or other outdoor activities.

Left: Ski in/ski out facilities.

Below left: Lounge.

Below right: Exterior against Beaver Creek Mountain.

Photography: Hill Glazier Architects.

HKS Inc.

1919 McKinney Avenue
Dallas, TX 75201
214.969.5599
214.969.3397 (Fax)
www.hksinc.com

HKS Inc.

Las Ventanas Al Paraiso
Los Cabos, Mexico

Where seafarers once found safe harbor, the Los Cabos ("the Capes") region of Mexico's Southern Baja Peninsula now extends a warm welcome to vacationers seeking its sandy beaches, desert landscape, premier golf courses, and superb sport fishing and water sports. A unique way to enjoy the region's relaxed and low-key charms is at Las Ventanas Al Paraiso, a new, 64-key, 110-condominium, 288,000-square foot resort designed by HKS Inc. Literally a "Window to Paradise," Las Ventanas shelters guests in an intimate village of handcrafted, two-story, off-white stucco buildings connected by stairs, bridges and curving paths that are adorned with desert flowers and palm trees and surrounded by the sparkling Sea of Cortez. With golf, tennis, yachting and other leisure diversions complemented by a world-class Spa, well-equipped Conference Center, Wine Room serving Baja-Mediterranean cuisine and Sea Grill interpreting traditional Mexican dishes, Las Ventanas offers a wealth of experiences the travelers of yesteryear could only have dreamt about.

HKS Inc.

Four Seasons Inn &
Conference Center
Irving, Texas

Working hard and playing hard are part of the good life in greater Dallas, which is why the new Four Seasons Inn & Conference Center in Irving has quickly become a favorite of residents and visitors alike. The handsome, 315-room, 10-story, 430,000-square foot hotel on 25.6 acres in the heart of the North Texas hills, designed by HKS Inc., excels in blending work and play. The architecture pays homage to the traditional styles favored by the region with cornices, arched windows, brick walls and tile roofs. Indoors, guests get down to business in 26 conference rooms with advanced audio-visual technology, an amphitheater with tiered seating, multi-purpose ballroom, communication resource center and guestrooms with computer links and closed circuit TV for monitoring meetings. After work, two championship golf courses, full-service spa, tennis courts, swimming pools, beauty salon and three restaurants let guests choose their own perfect ending for the day.

Above: Casitas and golf course.

Right: Main building.

Below: Serpentine pool.

Opposite lower left: Amphitheater.

Opposite lower right: Restaurant.

Photography: Tom Fox.

HKS Inc.

Las Ventanas Sonoma
Sonoma, California

Picture a 98-room, 203,150-square foot, world-class resort where guests will reside in rustic cottages carefully tucked into the wooded slopes of a 55-acre site in California's magnificent Sonoma County, adjacent to the historic Chateau St. Jean winery. Then imagine a spa, guest club, tasting room and grill, restaurant, bar and private dining and conference facilities, arranged in a Tuscan-style village setting that will be timeless in design yet modern in comfort. A gourmet's dream? Las Ventanas Sonoma, designed by HKS Inc., will offer guests gourmet delights and more to savor. Justly famed for its award-winning wineries, Sonoma County also boasts a dramatic Pacific coastline, the winding Russian River, majestic old growth redwoods, thriving farms, artist-and-craftsman colonies and historic towns, just 35 miles north of San Francisco. Las Ventanas will quickly become the perfect place to taste it all.

Left: Restaurant and guest spa buildings.

Lower left: Executive retreat.

Lower right: Typical guest cottage encircled by mature oak trees.

Bottom right: View from the Chateau St. Jean patio.

Illustrations: Warren Pullen/HKS Inc.

135

HKS Inc.

Deer Crest Lodge
Deer Valley, Utah

Devotees of skiing and other winter sports need no prompting to head for Deer Valley, nestled in Utah's picturesque Rocky Mountain Wasatch Range, at the first sign of snow. Long recognized as one of the world's finest ski resort destinations, Deer Valley and Park City served as the official site of the 2002 Olympics Slalom, Mogul and Aerial events. The opening of Deer Crest Lodge, designed by HKS Inc., will embellish its reputation with a 130-key, ski-in and ski-out resort sited on a "saddle" between ski runs that will be connected to additional hotel buildings and guestrooms at the base of the Deer Hollow ski lift by a funicular. From its breathtaking views to its world-class accommodations and services, Deer Crest Lodge will give both Black Diamond and non-skiers year-round pleasures to experience.

Top left: The mid-mountain site of Deer Crest Lodge.

Upper left: The Lodge's grand hotel.

Above: The great room in the grand hotel.

Illustrations: Warren Pullen/HKS Inc., Henriksen Design Associates.

Jonathan Nehmer + Associates, Inc.

1300 Piccard Drive
Suite 100
Rockville, MD 20850
301.670.1635
301.670.9643 (Fax)
www.nehmer.com
jnehmer@nehmer.com

Jonathan Nehmer + Associates, Inc. Marriott Hotel Orlando-Lake Mary
Lake Mary, Florida

Central Florida has not been the same since Mickey Mouse opened his Orlando residence to the world in 1971. Yet metropolitan Orlando is not wholly defined by such tourist attractions as Universal Studios, Sea World or Walt Disney World, since neighboring communities are pursuing their own economic destiny. The recent opening of the Marriott Orlando-Lake Mary, a 304-room, 10-story, 206,455-square foot hotel in Lake Mary designed by Jonathan Nehmer + Associates, attests to the bright prospects for Seminole County, home to 379,278 residents and one of Florida's fastest growing areas. The hotel serves business travelers with an 11,800-square foot meeting space, 8,600-square foot ballroom, restaurant, lounge, fitness center, outdoor pool and guestrooms for work and relaxation, taking cues from local high-tech facilities to project a fresh, modern image that doesn't predictably proclaim, "Florida hotel."

Above left: Cobalt's Lounge.

Above right: Conference entrance.

Left: Lobby.

Far left: Board room.

Opposite: Bistro Fifteen-O-One.

Photography: Neil Rashba Photography.

Jonathan Nehmer + Associates, Inc. Wyndham Orlando Resort
Orlando, Florida

Above: "Gatorville" Pool Bar & Grill.

Right: Lobby and registration.

Left: Augustine's Bar.

Below: Guestroom.

Photography: Eric Kieley Photography, Art Beaulieu Photography, Mullen Advertising & Public Relations.

Guests at the 48-acre Wyndham Orlando Resort may marvel at how close the plantation-style resort is to Orlando's bustling International Drive, since the everyday world disappears once they turn in. Yet there's nothing mysterious about the Resort's appeal to families visiting Walt Disney World, Universal Studios and Sea World, thanks to the work of Jonathan Nehmer + Associates as master planner and architect of record. The remodeling and expansion, encompassing 19 one- and two-story buildings and 1,065 rooms, 25,000 square feet of meeting space, four restaurants, a Kids Klub and a pool bar/grill, is anchored by a new central mall and landscaping that give the site good orientation. Such delights as charming Family Fun Suites with bunk beds and play areas, recreational activities such as tennis, sauna, volleyball and swimming and wading pools, and shopping on-site and nearby provide the finishing touches to a perfect vacation.

Jonathan Nehmer + Associates, Inc.

Virginia Crossings Conference Resort
Glen Allen, Virginia

How would Thomas Jefferson have designed the gracious, new Virginia Crossings Conference Resort in Glen Allen? No matter what America's third president—and talented amateur architect—might have done, it's easy to imagine him enjoying the inspired conversion of a former corporate headquarters by Jonathan Nehmer + Associates. The 20-acre project, comprising the renovation of two office buildings, 36,528-square foot Madison Hall and 44,000-square foot Jefferson Hall, and the construction of a new, 183-room, 112,900-square foot, five-story guestroom building, combines "Living, Learning and Leisure" as seamlessly as possible. Everywhere guests venture within the complex, which includes a ballroom, restaurant, buffet and pre-function space in addition to conference facilities, they find elegant, Colonial-style interiors equipped with modern conveniences like telephones with data ports, voice mail and high-speed Internet access. When it's time for relaxation, magnificent flower gardens and such recreational activities as golf, swimming, racquetball and billiards make Virginia Crossings fit for a president.

Above left: Lobby, main registration, Jefferson Building.

Above right: Jefferson Building.

Opposite below left: Lounge.

Opposite below right: Guestroom.

Photography: Art Beaulieu Photography.

Jonathan Nehmer + Associates, Inc. Hershey Lodge & Convention Center
Hershey, Pennsylvania

You needn't be a child to have a sweet tooth, as children of all ages know. Even so, why are organizations sending people to Hershey, Pennsylvania, the "Sweetest Place on Earth" where families tour Milton S. Hershey's fabled candy business? Chocolate lovers or not, these travelers are checking into this new facility at the Hershey Lodge & Convention Center, designed by Jonathan Nehmer + Associates. Guests find doing business is a pleasure in the warmth, comfort and efficiency of the 231 new guestrooms on five floors, 30,000-square foot, three-story exhibit hall, two-story lobby building and two-story parking structure, all designed in turn-of-the-century Adirondack style. In fact, three restaurants, two lounges and such recreational facilities as swimming pools, saunas, exercise room and tennis courts can make your stay quite sweet. The new facility raises the total number of rooms at the resort to 665.

Left: Grand fireplace and dining area.

Bottom left: Porte-cochere.

Below: Lodge and Convention Center.

Bottom: Lobby and front desk area.

Photography: Eric Kieley Photography.

Looney & Associates

3131 McKinney Avenue
Suite 310
Dallas, TX 75204
214.720.4477
214.720.4478 (Fax)
www.looney-associates.com

162 West Hubbard
Suite 302
Chicago, IL 60610
312.329.0464
312.329.0469 (Fax)

Looney & Associates

The Woodlands Waterway Marriott Hotel & Convention Center
The Woodlands, Texas

Above: Entrance lobby.

Below: The 225-seat restaurant.

Top: Suite.

Right: Lounge.

Photography: Creative Resources, Inc.

The Woodlands Waterway has captivated residents of The Woodlands, a 27,000-acre master-planned community 27 miles north of Houston, since plans were announced for the 1.25-mile long transportation corridor, linear park, and water feature linking offices, shopping, dining, residences, parks and entertainment venues in The Woodlands Town Center. It's quite understandable, given the beauty of the meandering river within the wooded site, and the bold, contemporary architecture of the new, 435,000-square foot Woodlands Waterway Marriott Hotel and Convention Center. The hotel indulges guests with relaxed, elegant interiors by Looney & Associates that include 352 guestrooms, 70,000-square foot convention center, lobby, restaurant, bar, health club and concierge lounge, furnished with natural materials, rich colors and—of course—waterway views.

Rising like a phoenix from the banks of the Tennessee River in the southern Appalachian Mountains, Chattanooga is a gracious Southern city that has saved its 19th-century heritage, breathtaking landscape and business vitality from urban blight. One of the most visible new symbols of its renaissance is The Chattanoogan, a 210,000-square foot conference center and hotel at the center of the burgeoning Southside district. The four-star hotel beside the 24,000-square foot conference center offers 215 guestrooms, 20 meeting rooms, a restaurant and banquet facilities, two private dining rooms and a parking garage for over 1000 vehicles, framed by an architecture of masonry and exposed steel trusses recalling Chattanooga's great steel foundries and other industrial structures. Inside, the interior design by Looney & Associates combines brick, stone, steel and wood with fine fabrics, finishes and res-

idential-style furniture as well as commissioned art from Tennessee artists to sustain a warm, inviting feeling that should draw business people to Chattanooga for years to come.

Above: Bar at Tuscany's restaurant.

Left: Lobby entrance.

Below: Tuscany's restaurant.

Bottom: Suite.

Photography: Mark Knight.

Looney & Associates

Westin Riverwalk
San Antonio, Texas

If you miss the Riverwalk, San Antonians say, you miss San Antonio. Though another local attraction remains the most popular place in Texas—the Alamo, where Davy Crockett, Jim Bowie and 188 compatriots fell to Mexican General Santa Anna in 1836—the heavily landscaped, 2-1/2-mile long Paseo Del Rio, a picturesque waterway lined by restaurants, hotels and shops, is universally loved. For the graceful, new, 375,000-square foot, 476-room Westin Riverwalk, designed by Looney & Associates, direct river frontage is an obvious source of inspiration. However, the hotel, which includes lobby, restaurant, bar, ballroom, junior ballroom, meeting rooms, health club, pool and terrace as well as guestrooms and suites on three public floors and 13 guestroom floors, offers more. Guests see tra-

Below left: Lobby reception.

Opposite: Staircase to public areas.

Photography: Mark Knight

ditional Mexican art and artifacts combined with handcrafted furnishings of various regional styles within an interior architecture of hand-applied stucco, Texas limestone, Mexican travertine, weathered iron, Venetian plaster, mahogany and marble that evokes a classic Texas estate. It's decidedly more hospitable than the Alamo—even for San Antonians.

Marnell Architecture & Interior Design

222 Via Marnell Way
Las Vegas, NV 89119
702.739.2000
702.739.2005 (Fax)
www.marnellcorrao.com

Marnell Architecture & Interior Design

Marnell Architecture & Interior Design

Panevino Ristorante & Gourmet Deli
Las Vegas, Nevada

Above left: Bar area.

Above right: Delicatessen.

Below right: Bar and lounge.

Opposite: Dining area.

Photography: Darius Kuzmickas.

Jaded citizens of Las Vegas surprised themselves recently when Panevino Ristorante & Gourmet Deli opened its doors. The new, 20,000-square foot Italian restaurant, designed by Marnell Architecture & Interior Design, promptly began turning heads with its distinctive architecture of rusticated travertine walls, a tilted and undulating horizontal band of glass overlooking The Strip and McCarran Airport, and refined detailing that includes bronze hardware, hardwood casework and custom lighting fixtures of Murano glass. Its 278-seat dining room, 174-seat bar and lounge, banquet/meeting rooms seating 167, and a separate 65-seat delicatessen represent an ambitious scheme that accommodates business events as well as traditional table service guests. Happily, customers report that with such highlights as two versions of carpaccio and grilled quail topped with a port wine sauce among the antipasti, and cioppino, osso buco, swordfish rolled and stuffed with crab and asparagus, and ravioli filled with lamb and topped with wild mushroom sauce and fresh rosemary as entrees, the menu measures up to the architecture in a city that is fast learning to take both seriously.

Marnell Architecture & Interior Design

Harrah's Bayview Tower
Grand Lobby and Dignitary Suites
Atlantic City, New Jersey

While Harrah's Atlantic City has always offered gaming action for everyone, from nickel slot machines to exclusive table games, its facilities have been relatively modest in appearance. Now, thanks to a new, 31,000-square foot grand lobby, featuring a spacious dome and three monumental aquariums, and a new addition to the 1,626-room hotel, the 25-story Bayview Tower, showcasing four 3,000-square foot Dignitary Suites appointed in marble, mahogany, platinum leaf and silk wall upholstery, both projects designed by Marnell Interior Design, the hotel offers the grandeur and ele-

gance demanded by the most affluent guests. In a setting that includes a promenade, registration, "Club Cappuccino" coffee shop and VIP registration, Harrah's Atlantic City is drawing exactly the kind of attention it wants.

Above left: One of three aquariums.

Above right: Living room in a Dignitary Suite.

Right: Dignitary Suite showing fireplace.

Below right: Dining room in Dignitary Suite.

Opposite: Dome in grand lobby.

Photography: Darius Kuzmickas.

Marnell Architecture & Interior Design

Palazzo Suites at The Rio
Las Vegas, Nevada

High rollers are the aristocrats of gaming, and the accommodations and services they receive in return for patronage that may amount to six- and seven-figure accounts are legendary if invisible to the public. The recently completed Palazzo suites at the all-suite Rio Hotel & Casino in Las Vegas, for example, add nine luxury suites ranging from 5,000 to 13,500 square feet in size, totaling 123,000 square feet on four floors. Each Palazzo suite, designed as a unique environment by Marnell Architecture & Interior Design, offers a private pool area, bar, atrium and garden as part of a generous apartment appointed in mahogany, marble, gold leaf, wool, silk and a lavish assortment of custom furnishings, including 17th-century Italian tapestries and works by artists Jasper Johns and Richard Diebenkorn. Every convenience is thoughtfully provided, including Internet service for computer-literate tycoons who wish to combine gaming and surfing.

Top right: The Rio Hotel & Casino.

Upper and lower right: Interiors of various Palazzo suites.

Opposite: Palazzo suite entry hall and living room.

Photography: Ed Masterson.

Marnell Architecture & Interior Design

Fiore
Harrah's Shreveport
Shreveport, Louisiana

You don't have to be big to win in gaming, and Harrah's Shreveport Casino, a stationary boat with a 23,000-square foot casino, four restaurants and a 514-room hotel, thrives in the competitive Shreveport market through top quality. The 4,000-square foot, 160-seat Fiore steakhouse, designed by Marnell Architecture & Interior Design, draws crowds to its fine dining using modern design.

Instead of the aggressively masculine milieu steakhouses exude, Fiore envelopes guests in a graceful, elegant setting of light, bleached movingui wood, custom Murano glass fixtures, linen wall fabric, wool carpet, marble, gold leaf, elegant, contemporary furnishings and fine art to add the finishing touch to a delectable visit.

Upper left: Sculpture in the dining room.

Left: Detail of ceiling cove.

Above: Entrance and reception.

Photography: Darius Kuzmickas.

Marve Cooper Design, LLC*

2120 W. Grand Avenue
Chicago, IL 60612
312.733.5159
312.666.3018 (Fax)
www.marvecooperdesign.net

* Formerly Lieber Cooper Associates

Marve Cooper Design, LLC

Fogo de Chao
Chicago, Illinois

America's enduring appetite for steaks, chops and other choice cuts of meat has been intriguingly stimulated by the introduction of "Churrascaria," the Brazilian way of slow roasting meat over an open wood flame, in Dallas, Houston, Atlanta and Chicago, by Sao Paolo-based Fogo de Chao. The restaurant group's latest opening in America is the Windy City's new, 12,500 square foot, 350 seat restaurant at 661 North LaSalle, designed by Marve Cooper Design. Churrascaria, a three-century old culinary tradition among the "gauchos" or cowboys of the Rio Grande do Sul region in southern Brazil, became a winning concept for the Coser and Ongaratto brothers when the restaurateurs founded Fogo de Chao in 1979 and opened their first restaurant in Sao Paolo. Their modus operandi contrasts with that of the traditional U.S. steakhouse. Instead of inviting guests to place orders for separate main courses, Fogo de Chao welcomes them to sample any or all of 15 selections of beef, lamb, pork and chicken that waiters serve tableside for a fixed price. Cooper has established a lively

Above left: Fogo de Chao restaurants are distinguished by the "fire in the earth", a literal translation of the name, and a chimney. Below is a glassed-in rotisserie set in limestone with color-graduated ceramic tiles..

Left: Bar/waiting area uses granite, wrought iron, slab glass, and polished woods is set apart from the dining rooms, but reflect their relationship..

Opposite: "Waterfall wall" with stylized timbers in main dining room allude to the Brazilian rainforest. Dining room has slate flooring, wrought-iron/burnished-wood partitions and hand-cast stained-glass/metal chandeliers.

sequence of rustic spaces to introduce guests to this exotic world. Two dramatically designed areas of display and activity, including the glassed-in, flame-licked rotisserie of limestone and ceramic tile at the entrance and the elegant wood-trimmed salad bar and wrap-around wine display in the main dining room, attract guests' attention before they proceed to their tables in one of three robust dining rooms (one for private parties) appointed in wood, plaster and ceramic tile to surrender themselves to a carnivore's movable feast.

Above: A 35-ft. mural depicting the lifestyle of the Brazilian gaucho country and customs provide a focal point for the private dining room. Glass/ stone walls, chandeliers and fireplace reflect the naturalness of the region.

Opposite above and below: Spectacular salad bar adorned with fresh flowers and lit from above with slatted wood shutters.. Opposite salad bar is wraparound wine room. Patrons pass the wine and salad displays on their way to two a la carte dining rooms.

Photography: Mark Ballogg, Steinkamp-Ballogg.

Marve Cooper Design, LLC

Aria
Chicago, Illinois

Above: A revolving door entry foreshadows the unity of the interior design. Changing colors in circles flanking logo are computer controlled

Right: Cocktail area with rounded-arm seating, circular tables, and upholstered banquette wall topped by photomural celebrating the art of dance and music.

Photography: Mark Ballogg, Steinkamp-Ballogg.

Hoteliers are understandably thrilled when their restaurants win acclaim from food critics and travel guides, and the Fairmont Hotel Chicago is no exception, now that the new, 206 seat, 9,050 square foot Aria Restaurant & Bar has been hailed for the delectable cuisine from chef James Wierzelewski, courteous service from the staff and elegant interior from the Marve Cooper Design team. Of course, the chef was singled out for such innovative, Asian and European-influenced creations as pan-roasted osaka black cod, zinfandel braised beef short ribs, and star anise lacquered baby chicken. Yet the curvilinear forms, intricate ceilings and dramatic lighting of this clean, modern setting won kudos for their impressive ability to turn an irregular and angular space into a sleek and stylish restaurant that the Chicago Tribune called "elegantly down to earths."

Top left: Wine display is glassed to show cylindrical bottle ends. The circular chef's action station, food displayed and tandory oven continue the curvilinear theme.

Left: Connections between rooms are anchored with circularity at there ends. Arch-shaped coffers, curved wall sconces, and rounded alcoves containg the cheif's table diminish the corridor's straightness.

MBH Architects

1115 Atlantic Avenue
Alameda, CA 94501
510.856.8663
510.865.1611 (Fax)

www.mbharch.com

1300 Dove Street
Suite 100
Newport Beach, CA 92660
949.757.3240
949.757.3290 (Fax)

MBH Architects

MBH Architects
P.F. Chang's China Bistro

P.F. Chang's China Bistro at the
Aladdin Hotel
Las Vegas, Nevada

When a contemporary Chinese-influenced restaurant encounters a Hollywood-style, Arabic-themed resort, the result is the kind of cultural encounter that gives Las Vegas its unmistakable energy and raw appeal. The impact is unmistakable in the new, 14,000-square foot, two-level, 219-seat P.F. Chang's China Bistro at the Aladdin Resort & Casino. Designed by MBH Architects and P.F. Chang's China Bistro's Design Director, Brian Stubstad, and built by ITX Construction, this Chang's stretches a thematic bridge between the two milieus. While the restaurant occupies a long, narrow space sandwiched between the casino and the heavily themed facade, the dining room displays no sense of confinement as it soars to a double-height volume with upper-level dining areas on each end. The visual drama is extended by such careful detailing as fine fabric on dark wood dining chairs and banquettes, custom, six-foot-long pendant light fixtures of molded plywood and acrylic, an exquisitely crafted wood and glass staircase, cherry wood booths, stone wall tiles and brass hardware. For guests ordering such dishes as Chang's Spicy Chicken, Mongolian Beef or Cantonese Roasted Duck, this contemporary bistro has providing a most appetizing setting.

Above left: Bar.
Above right: Exterior elevations.
Left: Small dining room.
Opposite: Main dining room.
Photography: Andreas Brizzi.

MBH Architects

Shadow Ridge
Palm Desert, California

Left: Approach to Golf Club House.

Below left: Golf Club House main lobby.

Below right: Villas in Palm Desert.

Photography: Dennis Anderson.

What is life like in paradise? Residents of Palm Desert, California, a community of 42,350 permanent residents in Riverside County's sunny Coachella Valley, think they know. The sky is clear blue 350 days annually, the temperature ranges between January's 41-70 degrees and July's 74-107 degrees, and the local cultural and retail activities attract people from nearby La Quinta, Palm Springs and Rancho Mirage.

One of the latest attractions is Marriott's Shadow Ridge Villas at Palm Desert, designed by MBH Architects and built by R.D. Olson Construction and Sundt Construction. Shadow Ridge's one thousand 1,400-square foot dwelling units, housed in 30 distinct Villas, enjoy an 18-hole Nick Faldo Golf Course and Training Institute on a 312-acre site. Spectacular views of Mount San Gorgonio and Mount San Jacinto are enhanced with site planning, fountains and lakes, extensive grading and water movement. Indoors, the Villas offer spacious open layouts appointed in luxurious textiles and comfortable furnishings that are just perfect for paradise.

MBH Architects

Newport Coast Villas
Newport Beach, California

Many vacationers have been seduced by the sight of Newport Coast Villas, a new vacation ownership property from Marriott that rises dramatically from sloping terrain overlooking the Pacific Ocean in Newport Beach, California. And why not? As designed by MBH Architects with WATG and HRP LanDesign, and built by R.D. Olson Construction, the award-winning, 75-acre ensemble resembles a timeless, Tuscan-style hilltop village with 39 three- to five-story villas, housing some 700 two-bedroom, 1,250-square foot units, clustered around a central piazza with fountains, cascading pools, sculpture and numerous convenience shops. To make the vision complete, the villas and on-site spa, fitness center and other recreational amenities that accompany them are expressed in traditional, Mediterranean construction with prominently sited towers, stucco walls, tile roofs, arched windows and doorways, wood trellises and luxurious yet comfortable interiors, and set into a thriving landscape of olive and palm trees overlooking neighboring Catalina Island that makes the hectic, everyday world seem far away.

Above: A view of the villas and spa from the piazza.

Below: Main lobby of the spa.

Opposite: One of numerous towers.

Photography: Dennis Anderson.

MBH Architects

MoMo's San Francisco Grill
San Francisco, California

Whether they see fine dining as a contact sport or a cultural event, San Francisans take haute cuisine seriously, and their pleasure at finding it just a stolen base from the home of the San Francisco Giants has spelled immediate success for MoMo's San Francisco Grill. Located at 760 Second Street across from PacBell Park, 260-seat Momo's features indoor dining, bar and outdoor seating in a handsome Arts & Crafts space with exposed rafters, warm earth tones and historic city photos on the walls, created by MBH Architects and Cannon Construction from a former printing warehouse for restaurateur Peter Osborne, owner of Washington Square Bar & Grill. For what CNN's Phil Taylor calls "delicious food" from an "unpretentious menu," including such entrees as Oven Roasted Halibut with a Sweet Thai Chili Sauce, Dijon Crusted Rack of Lamb with Rosemary Potatoes or Porcini Mushroom and Ricotta Cheese Ravioli Bolognese, Momo's easily wins its MVP.

Above left: One of two private dining rooms.

Above right: Projected vestibule entrance.

Right: Bar.

Photography: Dennis Anderson.

Mojo·Stumer Associates, P.C.

14 Plaza Road
Greenvale, NY 11548
516.625.3344
516.625.3418 (Fax)
www.mojostumer.com

Mojo•Stumer Associates, P.C.

Boca Rio Golf Club
Boca Raton, Florida

Serious golfers know Boca Raton's Boca Rio Golf Club, established in 1967, as an extremely challenging course, thanks to a masterful design by Robert von Hagge in 1967 that he updated in 1992, resulting in 195 acres of undulating greens, well bunkered and tree lined fairways, and a reasonable number of water hazards. Recently, the existing club house was updated to match the quality of the course through an award-winning renovation of 9,500 square feet of the 18,000-square foot structure by Mojo•Stumer Associates. The goal of the project, which involved the reception area, main gallery, lounge, bar, dining room and card room, was to transform a tired space into a more contemporary, sophisticated and warmer environment. The first step was to give the commercial-looking exterior a more residential appearance by exchanging the existing storefront windows for mahogany and glass units. Inside, every detail was scrutinized to create a fresh and exhilarating experience. For example, the stair from the main gallery to the locker rooms below was screened from immediate view by a ledge that served as a backdrop for the central seating area. Adding large sliding doors between the bar and card room allowed the bar to expand into the card room, introducing a

Above: Offices.

Below right: Card room.

Below left: Stairs from main gallery to locker rooms.

Opposite: Main gallery.

Photography: Brantley Photography.

lounge ambiance. Baffles were installed in the area between the dining area and back of the house services to soften the transition from the kitchen to the prep stations. A contemporary palette of warm and light materials and colors was devised to reflect Florida's climate. Even the phone booths received the same high degree of attention as everything else in a renovation that has drawn genuine praise from some of the Sunshine State's most demanding golfers.

Above: Bar seating area.

Left: Phone booth.

Far left: Woodworking details in lounge.

Opposite: Lounge.

Mojo·Stumer Associates, P.C.

EquinoxEquinox Fitness Club
New York, New York

You didn't have to be a fitness enthusiast or "health nut" to notice the difference. Equinox, a popular chain of fitness clubs, started out two decades ago looking nothing like the dreary establishments that typically catered to the physical culture crowd. From the moment it opened, Equinox demonstrated that there were better ways to encourage members to stay beyond the industry's usual three months than low prices or loud music. In fact, its combination of world-class trainers, state-of-the-art equipment and innovative fitness classes with cutting edge design and such amenities as a spa, cafe and store has succeeded in location after location. The power of this vision is showcased in a

Left: Entrance and two-story storefront.

Above right: Two-story entry corridor.

Top right: Reception desk and stairway.

Opposite: Indoor pool.

Photography: Phillip Ennis.

new, 35,000-square foot Equinox, designed by Mojo•Stumer Associates, on Manhattan's Second Avenue. The architect's award-winning fifth gym for Equinox overcomes an obvious handicap—most of its space is underground—by creating an open and airy setting. With its interior exposed behind a new, two-story glass exterior wall, the design establishes an feeling of spaciousness at street level that draws customers to the three lower levels, where sensitive floor plans, materials and lighting convince them to stay and bask in Equinox's glow.

Above: Exterior elevation.
Below left: Interior offices.
Below right: Product display niches.

Morris Nathanson Design

163 Exchange Street
Pawtucket
Rode Island 02860
401.723.3800
401.723.3813 (Fax)
www.morrisnathanson.com

Morris Nathanson Design

Morris Nathanson Design

Pine Hill Golf Club
Club House
Pine Hill, New Jersey

Left: Lounge with fireplace.

Above: Bar.

Below: Pro shop.

Opposite: Grille and Pub restaurant.

Photography: Warren Jagger.

A 20-minute drive from Philadelphia is all it takes to whisk serious golfers, their families and friends from everyday cares to the breathtaking Pine Hill Golf Club in Pine Hill, New Jersey, where fairways are lined by towering pine, oak, walnut and maple trees. Now, Club members have another compelling reason to attend, a new, 43,000-square foot, two-story Club House designed in the Arts and Crafts style by Morris Nathanson Design. Situated on southern New Jersey's highest elevation, the new facility offers a lobby, lounges, Grille and Pub restaurant, bar, ballroom, banquet rooms, locker rooms and pro shop in a gracious milieu combining modern convenience with traditional charm. Guests strolling along the wrap-around porches or gathering around a roaring fireplace can imagine themselves answering the call of the wild—with a good round of golf.

Morris Nathanson Design

Wequassett Inn
Chatham,
Massachusetts

Above: Fireplace in main dining room.

Left: Bar lounge.

Below: Main dining room.

Opposite: Pleasant Bay seen from the main dining room.

Photography: Warren Jagger.

New Englanders may revere their majestically austere landscape, but they clearly enjoy the world-class accommodations, dining and recreational activities at Cape Cod's venerable Wequassett Inn on Pleasant Bay. An enclave of cottages and colonial houses offering 104 guest rooms and public spaces, the Inn recently raised its sights with a sparkling, 4,200-square foot renovation by Morris Nathanson Design involving the dining room, private dining room, bar lounge and restrooms. Just as the Inn hoped, spectacular outdoor views, intriguing spatial arrangements, and updated classic furnishings in the new interiors are attracting guests from beyond the Inn.

Morris Nathanson Design

Mills Tavern
Providence, Rhode Island

Left: Private dining room.

Far left: Lounge dining.

Below left: Main dining room.

Opposite: View of open kitchen.

Photography: Warren Jagger.

The opening of Mills Tavern returns to Providence both popular chef Jaime D'Oliveira, who dazzled gourmets at other local restaurants, and 101 North Main Street, the historic Pilgrim Mills Building, a recent addition to downtown's ongoing revival. The 150-seat, bistro-style restaurant, which serves innovative American fare that changes with the seasons and the offerings of local purveyors, respects its historic context without copying it. Its unique blend of colonial and Arts & Crafts styles, created by Morris Nathanson Design, gives character to a 3,800-square foot space that is primarily open yet intimate in feeling, displays enormous windows and other hard surfaces without excessive reverberation, and encourages guests to share the entire fine dining experience with a fully open kitchen and chef's table for 12—a new restaurant poised to make history on its own.

Morris Nathanson Design

H^2O
Smithtown, New York

Long Islanders coming to the new H^2O restaurant in Smithtown, New York, for such seafood entrees as the 1950s-style shore dinner may be wondering where the standard displays of fish nets, lobster traps and harpoons are hidden. There's little nautical gear in sight. However, everyone immediately senses the exciting tastes and aromas of the sea that await them as they enter the 80-seat, 2,500-square foot, all-white space, designed by Morris Nathanson Design. The continuously flowing space captures the essence of naval architecture through the consistent use of horizontal vistas, employing such cues as bands of windows, arrays of framed prints, a long bar, rows of banquettes, and a private dining room framed by sliding doors. Of course, there are some model boats to remind landlubbers where they are.

Above: Main dining room.

Right: Private dining room.

Far right: Wait station.

Lower right: Bar.

Lower far right: Exterior and signage.

Photography: Warren Jagger.

Orlando Diaz-Azcuy Design Associates

Orlando Diaz-Azcuy
David T Oldroyd
Greg Stewart

201 Post Street
San Francisco, CA 94108
415.362.4500
415.788.2311 (Fax)
oda@odada.net

Orlando Diaz-Azcuy Design Associates

Courtside Athletic Club
Los Gatos, California

Passersby could easily ignore the Courtside Athletic Club in Los Gatos, California for decades—until now. With a recent renovation and addition by Orlando Diaz-Azcuy Design Associates as interior designer and DES Architects and Engineers as architect, the structure has emerged as a stylish country club. The 87,400-square foot transformation has doubled floor area and refurbished or introduced tennis courts, fitness center, spa, childcare facility, teen center, pools, conference center and cafeteria, using such basic materials as terracotta, cement, wood, stucco and simple, heavy casual furniture. How do the 3,000 members feel about the changes? They've retained Diaz-Azcuy for the last 25 years.

Above: Lobby and concierge desk.

Opposite: Facade.

Photography: Matthew Millman (above), John Sutton (opposite).

Orlando Diaz-Azcuy Design Associates

Pacific Athletic Club
San Diego, California

Take an ideal site for an athletic club, a varied building program including exercise rooms, aerobics room, gymnasium, tennis courts, child care center, conference center and lunch room/cafe, a gracious neighborhood and an almost perfect climate, and you have the striking new Pacific Athletic Club in San Diego, featuring an interior design by Orlando Diaz-Azcuy Design Associates. The fact that the client, Western Athletic Clubs, has been developing such facilities for 25 years helps explain the excellent layout of the two-story space. Yet the sweeping, contemporary interior design of stone floors, stone and plaster walls, bamboo screens and fine furnishings nearly overwhelmed the client, who declared, "It's very impressive."

Top: Entrance lobby.

Oposite: Main stair.

Photography: Toshi Yoshimi.

Orlando Diaz-Azcuy Design Associates

Horsley Bridge International
San Francisco, California and
London, United Kingdom

Above: Reception area, London.

Above right: Conference room,
San Francisco.

Opposite: Conference room,
London.

Photography: Matthew
Millman.

You can speak softly when you manage and invest billions of dollars in private business funds. Accordingly, Horsley Bridge International prefers understated, contemporary workplaces for employees and visitors rather than traditional, wood-paneled citadels of wealth. Its approach is aptly demonstrated in new installations in San Francisco and London, designed by Orlando Diaz-Azcuy Design Associates in a classic Modern vocabulary using such materials as Carrara marble, lacquer, birdseye maple, glass, carpet and furniture by the likes of Saarinen and Eames. For San Francisco, 40 employees occupy a 22,000-square foot, two-story space housing private offices, conference rooms, reception and lunch room inside a building whose curtain wall slants. The design tilts the ceiling up from core to perimeter to accentuate the geometry, promotes openness with casework and clerestory glass as perimeter partitions, and showcases an existing art collection. In London, the 3,500-square foot office includes private perimeter offices for all 12 employees plus an interior conference room, copy room-file storage and lunch room, responding to a scarcity of windows with frosted glass corridor walls and a California color scheme. For the firm that manages Horsley Bridge Partners, one of the world's largest private equity investors with over $6.2 billion of committed capital, speaking softly in the office is an art.

Orlando Diaz-Azcuy Design Associates

Masa's Restaurant
San Francisco, California

San Francisco hails the reopening of Masa's, one of its most honored restaurants, serving a new menu from acclaimed chef Ron Siegel and a new 2,000-square foot interior from Orlando Diaz-Azcuy Design Associates. "Though the menus and the design signal a rebirth," Siegel explains, "Masa's still honors the original vision of chef Masataka Kobayashi to provide a truly amazing dining experience where contemporary French food, gracious service, and an elegant setting are all in sync." Even so, Masa's deep-red, Gilded Age look of 1983 has yielded to chocolate-brown walls, a white bar, white curtains, French toile chairs and a winning ambiance that's reassuring established patrons while attracting a younger clientele.

Photography: David Duncan Livingston.

Rink Reynolds Diamond Fisher Wilson PA

Riverplace Tower
1301 Riverplace Boulevard
Suite 500
Jacksonville, FL 32207
904.346.3156
904.346.0781(Fax)
www.rrdfw.com
office@rrdfw.com

Rink Reynolds Diamond Fisher Wilson PA

Rink Reynolds Diamond Fisher Wilson PA

Matthew's
Jacksonville, Florida

Below: Custom serving bar in dining room.

Opposite lower left: Booth and banquette seating.

Opposite upper right: Finely detailed booth.

Photography: Joseph Lapeyra Photography.

Haute cuisine being highly prized today, Matthew Medure, respected owner/chef of one of Jacksonville's newest restaurants, Matthew's, may be pleased that his sizzling fare has displaced cold cash with the opening of the 2,500-square foot, 50-seat space, designed by Rink Reynolds Diamond Fisher Wilson, in a former bank. Medure's acclaimed light Mediterranean cuisine certainly befits the handsome and largely open milieu, which combines an original terrazzo floor with such new elements as a display kitchen, chef's dining counter, wine storage/display, candle screen, booth seating and freestanding tables, as well as restrooms and back-of-the-house facilities. Not only does the design successfully house an upscale restaurant in a limited space, it does so with the panache of an entree like European turbot with glazed green beans, parsley root juice and squash.

Rink Reynolds Diamond Fisher Wilson PA

Restaurant Medure
Ponte Vedra Beach, Florida

Celebrated owner/chef Matthew Medure knows how to use an exhibition kitchen, which is why his new, 4,500-square foot, 110-seat Restaurant Medure, in Ponte Vedra Beach, Florida, revolves around one. But the chic urban setting designed by Rink Reynolds

Diamond Fisher Wilson reveals itself as subtly as Medure's cuisine, which features seafood cooked with Southern, Mediterranean, Asian and Middle Eastern influences. Guests proceed from a lounge with eclectic furniture, a bar with a large communal table, a screen of

oak branches and brushed aluminum and a promenade flanked by floor-to-ceiling, glass-enclosed wine cellars to enter a variety of formal dining areas of varying seating capacities, all under a 13-foot-high ceiling layered with floating soffits, beams and suspended lighting fix-

tures. The restaurant's numerous transparent, translucent and semi-opaque architectural elements then entice guests to return, see and taste more.

Above left: Central dining area.

Above right: Sheer curtain detail.

Right: Screen and wine cellars.
Opposite: Bar and booth seating.

Photography: Joseph Lapeyra Photography.

Rink Reynolds Diamond Fisher Wilson PA

Ponte Vedra Inn & Club
Ponte Vedra Beach, Florida

Long before 1950s TV entertainer Arthur Godfrey acquainted middle-class Americans with Florida's exotic allure, affluent tourists were already calling on Florida resorts like the Ponte Vedra Inn & Club, a Spanish Colonial-style, 221-room hotel built in 1928 20 miles southeast of Jacksonville. To assure that the Inn attain top ratings, Rink Reynolds Diamond Fisher Wilson directed a massive renovation and expansion that refocused the much altered hotel on its roots in turn-of-the-century architecture, epitomized by the work of fabled architect Addison Mizner. Besides updating such existing areas as the lounges, bathrooms and courtyards, the architect has created new facilities for the lobby, retail shops, meeting rooms and guestrooms. Not only has the Inn's renaissance won various design awards, it received the coveted AAA Five-Diamond Rating in 2002.

Right: Great Room.

Below left: Lobby and mezzanine.

Below right: Retail shops.

Opposite: Fireplace in Great Room.

Photography: Dan Forer/Forer Incorporated.

Rink Reynolds Diamond Fisher Wilson PA

Gallery Bistro
Jacksonville, Florida

Diners in Jacksonville, Florida who like having such entrees as lobster and shrimp margarita pasta, gorgonzola stuffed filet with lobster ravioli, or wood grilled bourbon New York strip steak, a choice selection from an extensive wine list, and exquisite desserts served with live entertainment are discovering Gallery Bistro, a new, 6,000-square foot, 250-seat restaurant designed by Rink Reynolds Diamond Fisher Wilson. The split plan dining rooms on either side of the full-service bar allow the restaurant to operate multiple environments that serve guests comfortably whether they are arriving for drinks and socializing or for complete dinners. Every detail has been studied to give guests a memorable experience, right down to such visible features as the custom furniture and millwork, original artwork, and other hallmarks of a bistro that's both delicious and entertaining.

Above right: Wine cellar.
Right: Entry and bar.
Below: A quiet corner.
Photography: Joseph Lapeyra Photography.

SFA Design

5383 Hollister Avenue
Suite 260
Santa Barbara, CA 93111
805.692.1948
805.692.9293 (Fax)
www.sfadesign.com

130 South Harper
Los Angeles, CA 90048
323.651.2426
323.651.2436 (Fax)

SFA Design

SFA Design

Radisson Plaza Hotel Minneapolis
Minneapolis, Minnesota

Minnesota's cold climate is well-known, just as it must have been to the founders of Radisson Hotels & Resorts, who opened the first Radisson Hotel (honoring French 17th century explorer Pierre Esprit Radisson) in Minneapolis in 1909. Tempering the climate's impact has certainly been a goal, along with raising the standards of comfort and aesthetics, in the recent renovation of the 360-room, 16-story Radisson Plaza Hotel Minneapolis, the chain's flagship, which stands on the site of the original Radisson. As a result, the lobby and guest rooms have shed their traditional business décor for a contemporary ambiance with a custom boutique aura, as well as created additional meeting space and a new restaurant, the Fire Lake Grill House & Cocktail Bar. The lighter, brighter materials, such as

Above left: The restaurant's banquette seating.

Left: Counter service in the restaurant.

Above right: Registration and concierge.

Right: Suite living room and bedroom.

Photography: Jim Gallop, Gallop Studio.

warm woods, stone, satin nickel and brass, a rich color palette of amber, copper, tangerine and sea foam, Neoclassical furnishings and dramatic lighting are working their magic on the facility. This is the chain's flagship, which stands on the site of the original Radisson and is part of Plaza VII, a mixed use development completed in 1996. Notes an appreciative James Callaghan, general manager of the Radisson Plaza Hotel Minneapolis, "All of the new changes will enable us to provide the highest quality product and service for today's travelers, and maintains our position as one of the leading hotels in the market."

SFA Design

Park Towers
Las Vegas, Nevada

Luxury accommodations are among life's necessities in Las Vegas, where VIP guests are indulged in proportion to their house accounts, and the new Park Towers, a luxury, high-rise condominium of 84 apartments in two 20-story towers overlooking the Strip's "Golden Mile," is a formidable example. Residents enjoy panoramic views of the Strip's architecture and the valley's surrounding mountains from the balconies of two- or four-bedroom residences provided with state-of-the-art kitchens, baths and controls, semi-private elevators and assigned parking spaces. No less important are more than 30,000 square feet of public areas, designed by SFA Design to give an Old World ambiance to the lobby, billiards room, game room, theater, library, wine cellar, spa and business center that residents enjoy. Stretching a four-star budget to achieve a five-star level of finish, SFA Design has endowed the facilities with a rich, Italianate aura furnished with select hardwood veneers, fine fabrics, mosaic tile, marble and period-style furnishings. Simultaneously warm, spacious and modern, Park Towers dresses its part in Las Vegas life.

Above left: Library.
Left: Spa dressing room.
Far left: Spa whirlpool.
Opposite: Lobby.
Photography: Jeffrey Green.

Left: View to the bedroom.
Above: Living/dining area.
Below: Bedroom.

Many a leisure or business traveler has sampled the best New York City has to offer from the comfort and convenience of the Hilton New York at 1335 Avenue of the Americas, which recently completed a sweeping, $90 million renovation and redesign. Now it is possible for them to own a piece of their favorite lodging, just a few short steps from Fifth Avenue's famous shops and Broadway's glamorous theaters in Rockefeller Center, the heart of the nation's business and media center. To prepare the Hilton New York to welcome the Hilton Club, a new real estate product that combines vacation ownership in urban markets with members-only high-end services and exclusive travel privileges, SFA Design

remodeled two floors to incorporate an array of 78 studio, one- and two-bedroom units served by a members lounge, sales center, corridors and elevator lobbies. The attractive, new interiors are appointed in sleek, contemporary furnishings, including extensive, built-in furniture that saves space and reduces cost. At the Hilton Club, that is.

Above: Studio.

Right: Vignettes from various apartments.

SOSH Architects

1020 Atlantic Avenue
Atlanic City, NJ 08401
609.345.5222
609.345.7486 (Fax)
www.sosharch.com

Plaza 57
145 West 57 Street
New York, NY 10019
212.246.2770
212.246.2771 (Fax)

SOSH Architects

It's hard to imagine Palm Springs before the southern California desert community was "discovered" in the 1930s by such Hollywood celebrities as Lucille Ball, Jack Benny, Frank Sinatra and Bob Hope. A sign of the times is the impressive 200,000-square foot renovation and expansion of Trump 29 Casino, created for the 29 Palms Band of Mission Indians by SOSH Architects. Facing competing tribal casinos, the architects tapped two potent design themes: local architecture of the 1950s and 1960s, the object of current nostalgia, and natural splendors of the Coachella Valley, where Palm Springs resides. The completion of a new casino, premium player areas, restaurants, retail shops and a 2,500-seat theater has strongly reasserted Trump 29's presence. Its period-style architecture, which captures the "atomic age" optimism of the Eisenhower and Kennedy years, dramatically plays off such naturalistic imagery as a wall of fire behind a 25-foot column of falling water in the casino. As an example of the care that went into this project, the casino was not closed even for a day.

Top Left: Rattlesnake Lounge.
Opposite: Casino.
Bottom Left: Blue Lounge.
Bottom: Exterior.
Photography: Wayne Cable,
David Glomb

SOSH Architects

Brighton Steakhouse
Sands Casino Hotel
Atlantic City, New Jersey

Steakhouses usually mimic a Wild West ranch or a downtown men's club. However, the recent renovation of the 100-seat, Brighton Steakhouse at the Sands Casino Hotel in Atlantic City, designed by SOSH Architects, opens an alternative path to beefeater's heaven. The stylishly tailored design exploits its gallery-type space by running two rows of angled tables along the long walls, two rows of angled banquettes on either side of the long axis, and two six-place tables on the long axis. In a contemporary interpretation of Venetian carnival motifs, crisp diamonds on the ceiling and furniture plan play against stripes on the carpet, swirling patterns in the upholstery, and organic shapes in the wrought iron and blown glass chandeliers. Steak should look this appetizing.

Above: Window seating.

Left: Banquette view.

Opposite: Long axis perspective.

Photography: George Pierce Photography

SOSH Architects

ESPN Zone
New York, New York

How precious is commercial space in New York's Times Square? Ask Disney Regional Entertainment (DRE), which retained SOSH Architects to fit a 42,000-square foot ESPN Zone for sports-themed entertainment, shopping and dining into a building shell with a 10,000-square foot floor plate. ESPN Zone's indoor activities, including such interactive games and atractions as MoCap Golf, ESPN Bowling, Alpine Surfer and Daytona 2 Deluxe, typically combine physical exertion with computer simulation in a relatively modest amount of space. Still, SOSH has had to stack activities on multiple levels, deftly using floor cut-outs to reveal each level to visitors, and enticing visitors to visit everything via an open, airy staircase. Guests may not care that the space subtly disguises massive, 60-foot columns or isolates major sources of noise or vibration. However, DRE has taken notice—by entrusting more ESPN Zone work to SOSH.

Left: Exterior.

Above left: Staircase.

Photography: Norman McGrath.

Left: A SportsCenter attraction.

Above: Two-level space created by cut-out.

SOSH Architects

Swingers Lounge
Sands Casino Hotel
Atlantic City, New Jersey

Variety is the spice of casino life, prompting casino operators to make every effort to keep patrons happy and focused by serving them rich menus of diversions. The new Swingers Lounge, designed by SOSH Architects for the Sand Casino Hotel, in Atlantic City, offers an innovative solution to this ongoing concern. Locating the 5,000-square foot, two-story facility—equipped with a stage for live performers, a lighted dance floor, two mini-stages and a bar, all facing a nine-foot by 16-foot video wall—in the center of the casino brings music, dancing or perhaps a moment to enjoy the spectacle with friends over drinks right where the action is. Not only does the lounge let patrons on the second floor view the casino, it extends the gaming through video poker terminals mounted in the bar's countertop.

Above: Bar and video wall.
Right: Lounge seating.

SWA Group

2200 Bridgeway   Sausalito
PO Box 5904   Laguna Beach
Sausalito, CA 94966   Houston
415.332.5100   Dallas
415.332.0719 (Fax)   San Francisco
www.swagroup.com

SWA Group

SWA Group

Beverly Hills Hotel
Beverly Hills, California

Above left: Olympic-size pool and cabanas.

Above right: An original garden off Sunset Boulevard.

Photography: Tom Fox.

A cherished oasis for Hollywood since 1912, the Beverly Hills Hotel recently completed a $100 million restoration which included a refurbishing of the 12-acre landscape by SWA Group, reviving the glory of the 203-room "Pink Palace" and its 21 private bungalows. The

landscape architect's challenge was to reconcile historic restoration of the original gardens with the installation of needed new facilities on a site encompassing the gardens surrounding the hotel, two new on-structure gardens, private spaces around the bungalows and new events gardens. A survey of the 800 existing plant species and the placement of major trees and plants was completed before construction began on the buildings so the award-winning design could replicate historic plantings with existing or similar plants.

Consequently, the transition from original to new is seamless indoors and out, and you can still summon butler service while admiring the grounds simply by touching a button.

Left and opposite bottom: Views of historic and new pathways and gardens.

SWA Group

Hyatt Regency Scottsdale at Gainey Ranch
Scottsdale, Arizona

Below: A majestic allee of date palms.

Photography: Gerry Campbell, Dixi Carrillo.

Frank Lloyd Wright's arrival in 1937 to establish his studio, Taliesin West, may have been a milestone for the master architect, but it represented one of many steps for Scottsdale, Arizona, from a citrus orchard with one resident in 1888 to a thriving satellite of Phoenix with 126,000 residents a century later. Now recognized as a major tourist and business destination, this city in the heart of the Sonoran Desert has embraced the new, 493-room Hyatt Regency Scottsdale at Gainey Ranch as one of its premier resorts. One reason why is its superb 28-acre oasis, designed by SWA Group. The award-winning landscape, offering 20,000 square feet of swimming pools, 28 fountains, 47 waterfalls, a water slide and a beach, acknowledges the desert by making minimal use of water and maximum use of desert plants wherever possible. The result is a series of grand spaces, water playgrounds, jogging paths, bicycling trails and garden courts that recall ancient South American

motifs, highlighted by lines of date palms extending from the hotel building towards the mountains, that enchant the guests.

Top: The natural lake beside the hotel.

Upper left: Vista from the hotel to the mountains.

Left: Illuminated fountain.

Lower left and above right: Water playground pavilions.

SWA Group

Las Ventanas al Paraíso
Cabo San Lucas, Mexico

Above: The resort pool.

Right: An aerial view of the wedge-shaped site.

Opposite top right and left: Some of the many pathways.

Photography: Tom Fox.

True to its name, Las Ventanas al Paraíso, the new, 61-suite resort in Mexico's Los Cabos region at the tip of the Baja Peninsula, has been frequently likened to a "window to paradise." In fact, its blend of Mexican architectural tradition and contemporary, world-class accommodations does rise like a timeless village from fine white sand along the intensely blue Sea of Cortez. SWA Group's award-winning landscape design for the resort celebrates the raw beauty of the Baja Peninsula through a creative use of indigenous plants, local building materials and

Mexican artisans to bring out the beauty inherent in the land. The arroyos carrying water from the mountains to the sea, for example, have inspired the resort pool design and the razor-sharp infinity pool edge that seems to merge with the ocean and the horizon, truly a "window to paradise" to behold.

SWA Group

Lucaya Beach Resort
Freeport, Grand Bahama Island

Even paradise can welcome a makeover, as the rebirth of the 52-acre, 1,400-room Lucaya Beach Resort at Freeport, Grand Bahama Island, ravishingly illustrates. The story begins with an evaluation of three 1950s-era hotels at Lucaya, a beach resort a few miles east of Freeport, the Bahamas' "second city" after Nassau. Two are renovated, the third is replaced by a new, high-rise structure, and a new Manor House, resembling an island-style home, is developed for check in, departure and conveyance to the hotels, all within a landscape designed by SWA Group. Each hotel embodies its own theme and activities, using new pool and deck areas, restaurants, sports bars, food stands and support facilities. As a finishing touch, the landscape combines local plant materials and existing site trees with boldly colored, patterned and textured materials to give the resort the rich patina of a well-established Bahamian residence.

Left top: Manor House.

Left center: A gazebo on the connecting pathways.

Left bottom: Aerial view of the 52-acre site.

Below: Monumental planter.

Bottom: The beach.

Photography: Tom Fox.

URS Corporation

3950 Sparks Drive SE
Grand Rapids, MI 49546
616.574.8500
616.574.8542 (Fax)
www.urs.com

URS Corporation

AH! Mooré Gourmet Coffee & Bakery
Country Creek Commons
Rochester Hills, Michigan

He was one of the NFL's finest wide receivers, combining athleticism, grace and strength to capture passes above hordes of defensive backs. In eleven years with the Detroit Lions, 1991-2001, Herman Moore, a University of Virginia football and track star, became one of only two NFL players (with Jerry Rice) to play three consecutive seasons of 100 or more receptions. But after being released by the Lions in June 2002 and called late in the 2002-2003 season by the New York Giants without a starting position, Moore became a player without a team. What does a professional athlete do when the cheering stops? Moore wisely answered this question years earlier: food franchising. Yet his strategy has gone beyond buying Cinnabon stores with the founding of AH!Mooré Gourmet Coffee & Bakery, named for his wife Angela and himself. Convinced the coffee and bakery shop market has a good decade of growth left, he recently

Left: Lounge space and fireplace.

Right: Service counter with pastry cases.

Photography: Beth Singer.

located a 4,000-square foot, AH! Mooré at Country Creek Commons, in Rochester Hills, Michigan, to offer guests coffee, cappuccino, expresso, fine pastries, signature soups, sandwiches and salads, and gourmet ice cream, all served in an elegant, high quality and comfortable space designed by URS Corporation. The design, characterized by high ceilings, architectural columns, exceptional use of lighting and a fireplace, appears to be connecting with the public just as Moore has—and the game has just begun for AH! Mooré.

Above: Freestanding display unit and self-service island.

Opposite: Coffee preparation and serving area.

URS Corporation

AH! Mooré Gourmet Coffee & Bakery
Ford Field Football Stadium
Detroit, Michigan

A little cinnamon with your cappuccino before kick-off? Suddenly sports fans in Detroit's Ford Field Football Stadium have a classy new alternative to standard stadium fare, thanks to the arrival of a 1,500-square foot, AH! Mooré Gourmet Coffee & Bakery, designed by URS Corporation. The distinctively stylish cafe is part of a business created by local hero Herman Moore, a celebrated wide receiver for the Detroit Lions from 1991 to 2001. Its design is clearly shaped by its location. Standing at the top of an escalator to the second level at Ford Field, AH! Mooré provides high visibility for stadium guests and stadium employees in the office suites adjacent to

Above: Common area seating and storefront.

Opposite: Service counter and art wall depicting Herman Moore as a Lion.

Photography: Beth Singer.

Below: Service counter with display case in the foreground and plasma screen and beverage dispensers in the background.

the space. Its glass storefront allows guests to view the available offerings—specialty coffees, pastries, soups, sandwiches, salads and ice cream—before they arrive at a rounded service counter, which is mirrored in an overhead soffit. Once they have placed their orders, facing a blue tiled wall (the color matches the store logo) outfitted with a plasma screen to monitor action in the stadium, four

POS stations at the counter send them quickly on their way. Ready for your scrimmage, Starbucks?

Wimberly Allison Tong & Goo

700 Bishop Street
Suite 1800
Honolulu, HI 96813
808.521.8888
808.521.3888 (Fax)
honolulu@watg.com

2260 University Drive
Newport Beach, CA 92660
949.574.8500
947.574.8550 (Fax)
newport@watg.com

4132 Del Rey Avenue
Los Angeles, CA 90292
310.577.6400
310.577.8400 (Fax)
losangeles@watg.com

3023 80th Avenue SE
Suite 201
Mercer Island, WA 98040
206.275.2822
206.275.0692 (Fax)
seattle@watg.com

719 Peachtree Road
Orlando, FL 32804
407.298.9484
407.298.9184 (Fax)
orlando@watg.com

Alexandra House
6 Little Portland Street
London W1W 7JE
44.207.906.6600
44.207.906.6660 (Fax)
london@watg.com

15 Scotts Road
#03-09/10 Thong Teck Building
Singapore 228218
65.6227.2618
65.6227.0650 (Fax)
singapore@watg.com

Wimberly Allison Tong & Goo

The Ritz-Carlton, Lake Las Vegas
Henderson, Nevada

Right: Poolside view of exterior.

Below: Bridge structure and Lake Las Vegas.

Bottom left: Italian garden and fountain.

Bottom center: Firenze Lobby Lounge.

Opposite bottom: Medici Café and Terrace.

Photography: Peter Malinowski/InSite Architectural Photography.

Could a majestic, Tuscan-style, bridge-like structure really be spanning a secluded lake somewhere in the western United States? It's not a mirage—it's the new, 357,000-square foot, 349-room Ritz-Carlton, Lake Las Vegas, in Henderson, Nevada, designed by Wimberly Allison Tong & Goo. Modeled after the fabled Pontevecchio in Florence, Italy, the luxury destination resort hotel is the centerpiece of a 2,605-acre integral development, MonteLago Village, that comprises a casino, retail village and luxury condominiums. Rich in architectural imagery as the Ritz-Carlton's facilities are, encompassing reception, lounge, three restaurants, a 30,000-square foot, two-story spa, 32,000-square foot conference center that includes two ballrooms and outdoor venues, guestrooms, formal Italian gardens and 36-hole championship golf course, everything fits in carefully with its desert landscape and neighboring buildings. Declares Ron Boeddeker, chairman of the hotel's developer, Transcontinental Holdings, "Every part of this hotel is beautiful."

Wimberly Allison Tong & Goo

The Lodge at Torrey Pines
La Jolla, California

Left: Entrance to a suite.

Below left: Exterior.

Below right: Views of the spa, guest living room and bedroom.

Opposite: Lobby lounge.

Photography: John Durant Photography.

The Cinderella effect of architectural renovation is nothing less than astonishing at The Lodge at Torrey Pines, in La Jolla, California. Asked to transform a 75-room, 1960s motel into a 175-room luxury resort in the Craftsman style, Wimberly Allison Tong & Goo has created an award-winning design that commands its six-and-a-half-acre site overlooking the Pacific Ocean, adjacent to the Torrey Pines Golf Course. An architectural vision inspired by the Pasadena houses of Charles and Henry Greene is complemented by Craftsman-era materials and furnishings—including authentic Stickley furniture—and contemporary amenities and technology, including high-speed Internet access and advanced telecommunications. The best qualities of past and present await guests in the Lodge's guestrooms, meeting facilities, restaurants and spa.

Wimberly Allison Tong & Goo

Pan Pacific Singapore
Singapore

Singapore's pride in the 784-room Pan Pacific Singapore, with its 35-story atrium originally designed by architect John Portman, prompted Wimberly Allison Tong & Goo to recognize the existing detailing when it transformed two high-level hotel floors into world-class executive accommodations, including a new express check-in/reception, bi-level business lounge and 44 new suites. By day, the business lounge and reception area highlight Singapore as a progressive nation with futuristic interiors of steel, glass, tile and modern furniture. At day's end, the suites let guests trade the region's heat and humidity for a cool urban resort of deep-toned colors and furnishings, refinished teak cabinetry and trim, and new contemporary furniture, including Herman Miller's Aeron Chair in each room for the globe-girdling executive.

Above: Living room in bi-level suite.

Right: Guest bathroom.

Opposite upper left: Check in/reception and business lounge.

Opposite lower left: Guestroom table desk and office chair ensemble, and guestroom bed and bedside furniture.

Photography: Peter Mealin Photography.

Wimberly Allison Tong & Goo

Marriott Ko Olina Beach Club
Honolulu, Hawaii

The request was made of Wimberly Allison Tong & Goo to design the interiors for the Marriott Ko Olina Beach Club, the Marriott's flagship Hawaiian property on the western shore of Oahu. Additionally, the job had to be done on a strict budget. The solution mutually agreed upon by client and design firm was that the design—covering the lobby, marketplace, pool bar, health club, public restrooms and 103 guest villas—would let the environment look sumptuous by highlighting feature areas and keeping the overall architecture strong and simple in the Hawaiian tradition. The award-winning project displays its handsome decorative features as if featured in scenes from stories shared by the guests.

Top left: Dining area in suite.
Above: Living room.
Top right: Bedroom.
Right: Public area. Photograph by Olivier Koning.
Photography: Courtesy Marriott Vacation Club International.

Wilson Associates

3811 Turtle Creek Boulevard
15th Floor
Dallas, TX 75219
214.521.6753
214.521.0207 (Fax)

141 Milton Street
Brooklyn, NY 11222
718.349.2945
718.349.2342 (Fax)

8383 Wilshire Boulevard
Suite 611
Beverly Hills, CA 90211
323.651.3234
323.852.4758 (Fax)

47 Scotts Road #02-01
Goldbell Towers
Singapore 228233
65.6735.0624
65.6735.3347 (Fax)

Woodmead Office Park
20 Saddle Drive
Woodmead, South Africa
27.11.656.2020
27.11.656.4040 (Fax)

119 Madang Road Suite 501
Xintlandi Plaza
Shanghai 200021, China
86.21.6387.0866
86.21.6387.0766 (Fax)

www.wilsonassc.com

Wilson & Associates

Four Seasons Cairo at the First Residence
Cairo, Egypt

To survey the Nile, Great Pyramids and lush canopy covering Cairo's ancient Zoological and Botanical Gardens from a five-star hotel—a privilege denied Napoleon in his early 19th-century invasion of Egypt—you must stay at the new, 273-room Four Seasons Cairo at the First Residence. The hotel, named for the prestigious, new mixed-use development it dominates, represents a masterly conversion by Wilson & Associates of a building constructed as a condominium. Besides compensating for existing public spaces that were small for a hotel, the design celebrates the French passion with pharonic Egypt in Napoleon's time, establishing a strong sense of history that transcends the newness of the First Residence. Thus, whether guests use the business center or the lobby living room, restaurant, library bar, tea lounge or health club, all furnished in period style with superb antiques, they enjoy intimate luxuries the Little Corsican never experienced in Cairo.

Above: Lobby living room.
Upper left: Restaurant.
Left: Guest bath.
Lower left: Guest living room.
Opposite: Fourth floor lobby.
Photography: Robert Miller.

Wilson & Associates

The Villas & Spa at Little Dix Bay
Virgin Gorda, British Virgin Islands

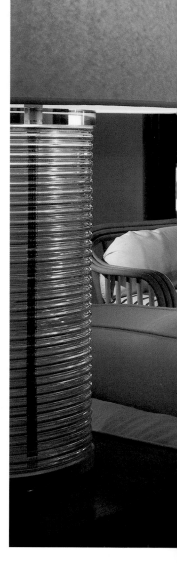

Vacationers who seek out the softly curving crescent beach of Little Dix Bay on the island of Virgin Gorda, in the British Virgin Islands, are often attracted by the unobtrusive presence of the resort's cottages and guestrooms. As envisioned by founder Laurance Rockefeller, the facilities offer a low-key luxury that respects the environment. Thus, the challenge for Wilson & Associates in adding a new spa and villas for four and six guests was to preserve Little Dix Bay's treasured privacy while offering unspoiled views to occupants of the new construction. The solution called for siting the new buildings so they are as discreetly woven into the landscape as their predecessors. Once guests enter the simple yet stylish interiors, featuring terra cotta clay tiles, plaster walls, timber ceilings and comfortable furnishings, Little Dix Bay feels like theirs alone.

Left: Exterior of spa.

Below left: Spa treatment room.

Below right: Dining al fresco.

Photography: Michael Wilson.

Above: Villa living room.
Left: Villa bedroom.

Wilson & Associates

Ritz-Carlton, Bachelor Gulch Hotel & Club
Bachelor Gulch, Colorado

Left: Grotto at spa.

Far left: Remington's Restaurant.

Below left: Fly fishing library.

Below right: The Buffalo Bar.

Opposite: Great Room.

Photography: Ken Redding Photography.

Today's ranchers may employ GPS in their airplanes and pickup trucks, but there are still places where the traditional image of the American West is nurtured with a devotion that might surprise native Westerners. The Ritz-Carlton, Bachelor Gulch, designed by Wilson & Associates, is a prime example. At this new, 237-room luxury ski resort, nestled in a quiet valley at the base of Beaver Creek Mountain in Bachelor Gulch, Colorado, 15 miles west of Vail, the only obvious 21st-century intrusions are its state-of-the-art conveniences. Guests enjoy ski-in/ski-out convenience, a 21,000-square-foot spa, 36 holes of golf, hiking, mountain biking, fly fishing and music festivals in a meticulously detailed setting that evokes the great lodges of the 1900s in America's National Parks. Whether they arrive for work or play, they have use of such facilities as the lobby lounge, library, restaurant, bar, spa, 1,500-square foot Ritz Kids activity center, five meeting rooms and ballroom. The surprise is that this extensive facility resembles a sumptuous private residence, appointed in authentic, handcrafted furnishings, rather than a grand hotel that could easily take its place with the Old Faithful Inn, Awahnee and Canyon Hotels of a century ago.

Wilson & Associates

Conrad Bangkok
Bangkok, Thailand

Business people and vacationers alike in Bangkok, the capital of Thailand, find themselves at home in the new Conrad Bangkok, a luxurious, 375-room business hotel designed by Wilson & Associates with all the trappings of a destination hotel. The hotel's dual nature reflects its location in the heart of Bangkok's business and embassy district—within walking distance of the U.S. Embassy, mass transit and such corporate powerhouses as General Electric, Merrill Lynch and Toyota, yet close to attractions like the Grand Palace and Temple of the Emerald Buddha. Its sophisticated contemporary Thai environment of silk, teak and custom furniture and carpets puts both executives and vacationers at ease in such facilities as the lobby lounge, restaurant, bar, ballroom, meeting rooms, health club and spa—an apt place to sample the city that Thais call "The City of Angels."

Above: Lobby.

Right: Lounge.

Far right: Sitting room.

Lower right: Guest bedroom.

Lower far right: Guest suite.

Photography: Courtesy of Conrad Bangkok.

BERGAMO IS. . .

ULF MORITZ
SAHCO HESSLEIN

By Roger Yee

Welcome Back!

An alert and eager crowd, smartly attired for business, started assembling long before the doors to the cheerful little breakfast cafe opened at Tokyo's sleek InterContinental Hotel in the Shinjuku district. The faces in the crowd were mostly American, and the reason they were so punctual was evident the moment they rushed into the bright, contemporary environment of wood, tile and stainless steel. The unmistakable odors of a hot U.S.-style breakfast—scrambled eggs, bacon, pancakes, coffee and other mainstays of mornings in America—had triggered a primal urge among people for whom a bowl of rice, a filet of smoked fish and a dish of pickled vegetables for breakfast might never seem routine.

*A*fter September 11, 2001, the world of business travel changed in ways veteran hoteliers suspect are both fundamental and irreversible.

It's a scene that took place some years ago, yet continues to replay itself in hotels and restaurants around the world. Hoteliers and restaurateurs prosper by giving guests what they want. As the global economy continues to regain strength, the hospitality industry is hard at work enticing intrepid travelers and diners to leave home and work for adventure, discovery or perhaps just a few hours of self-indulgence.

Their efforts are bearing tangible fruit. According to the American Hotel & Lodging Association, the innkeeping industry anticipates a 3.6 percent increase in U.S. hotel revenues by the end of 2003, representing a 7.8 percent increase in profits for the average U.S. hotel. It's not a bad showing for the nation's 47,040 hotels with 15 or more rooms, who collectively rang up $102.6 billion in sales and attained a 59.1 percent average occupany rate—just above the break-even rate for contemporary hotels—in 2002.

The National Restaurant Association predicts that restaurant industry sales should reach $426.1 billion in 2003, posting a 4.5 percent gain, or 1.8 percent when adjusted for inflation, an improvement over the 1.3 percent real increase reached in 2002 that the Association considers only modest. Even so, dining out already accounts for some 47 percent of every dollar spent on food. The plight of time-pressed consumers to find time to eat three proper meals a day has inspired almost one-third of new supermarkets to include casual dining-style restaurants, cafes or dining rooms, according to the Food Marketing Institute.

What women on business really want from a hotel

The gains are being secured by considerable effort, to be sure. The lodging industry, for example, saw business travel plummet immediately after September 11, 2001. Though corporate road warriors restarted their engines as soon as public anxiety subsided, the world of business travel changed in ways veteran hoteliers suspect are both fundamental and irreversible.

For example, organizations are frequently turning to teleconferencing and other electronic alternatives to routine meetings to save time, cost and risk, overcoming a deep-seated reluctance among their business managers to substitute high technology for traditional, face-to-face encounters. When corporate employees must hit the road, they are increasingly relying upon discount transportation carriers and value-oriented innkeepers to provide their services, bypassing travel agents to book these trips directly over the Internet. The savings are said to reach 15-20 percent on airline tickets alone. And while the elite of the business world continue to enjoy first-class travel, five-star hotels and four-star restaurants, their middle managers and junior executives are learning to rely on the likes of JetBlue, Days Inn, Olive Garden and the like.

To their credit, hotels are energetically striving to make business travel enjoyable again. Since business men and women are increasingly bringing spouses and children along for weekend vacations that commence once meetings conclude to reduce the cost of family vacations, which have been getting shorter and closer to home, business hotels are introducing such family-friendly amenities as spas, fitness and recreational facilities, and children's activity centers. Rising numbers of women traveling on business are also discovering that hotels not only offer room service when they wish to remain in their rooms, but also small, intimate dining rooms where individual guests can dine in comfort and privacy, beauty salons for physical and emotional renewal, and three- and four-star restaurants, often operated by independent restaurateurs, that allow women to entertain clients without having to leave their hotel. It's only a matter of time before hoteliers aggressively target senior citizens for special treatment.

*A*s for guests at resorts and casino hotels, hoteliers are introducing more activities to enrich their experience—and generate new income, such as shopping, fine dining and entertainment.

Hoteliers have made a night's stay easier on company accountants by lowering their break-even point through tighter operations and new facilities designed to extend the life cycle of materials, lower the cost of maintenance, economize on staffing and minimize energy consumption. Happily, their strategies include bold, new initiatives as well. Corporate travelers on tight budgets are discovering that "economy" and "midscale" hotels have thoughtfully added such business amenities as free continental breakfast and local phone calls, business and fitness centers, phones with dataports and wireless Web television. As for guests at resorts and casino hotels, hoteliers are introducing more activities to enrich their experience—and generate new income, such as shopping, fine dining and entertainment. Las Vegas has discovered that while tourists spend six times more on gaming than shopping, the amount they intend to spend on shopping is growing nearly three times faster than what they budget for gaming.

Ready for your red pepper pancakes with smoked salmon, caviar and creme fraiche?

Restaurateurs are also doing their part to remain busy and profitable by controlling expenses, tailoring menus to follow popular tastes and offering less costly menus amid attractive dining room settings. At the high end, fusion food, ethnic food from such novel sources as India, Vietnam, Argentina and Thailand, pasta in every variation, and healthy foods are finding their place at the dining table, along with "heirloom," "artisanal" and "organic" foods that are often proudly identified in menus as "potatoes from Maine," "Long Island duckling" and the like. The heightened sophistication of diners and the growing presence of new immigrant populations have also ushered new ingredients as well as new flavors into the kitchen. With choices for haute cuisine expanding in unprecedented ways, the traditional French, Italian, Chinese and American restaurants have even begun adding exotic entrees of their own to draw younger customers seeking "what's new."

More modestly priced establishments are striving to stretch customers' food budgets with price promotions while maintaining their interest with new flavors—hot and spicy is now becoming as commonplace in America as beefy and bland—or their opposite craving for the familiar flavors of comfort food. Fast-food ("quick-service" in industry parlance) restaurants are fighting an uphill struggle particularly at dinner time, as families turn to "quick-casual" restaurants for more interesting fare that arrives with reasonable prices in attractive and comfortable settings. Part of their problem is the saturation of the market for menus based on ground beef—note the efforts by McDonalds, Burger King and Wendy's to raise same-store sales—which is leading quick-service chains to experiment with new formats such as fresh salads, gourmet sandwiches and healthy fare.

Lighting to live with a $44 million art collection.

Nemacolin Woodlands, a world class resort and spa in Pennsylvania, contains a precious art collection that includes Remingtons, Ertés and original Audubon sketch books.

For this very unusual project, we produced custom crystal wall sconces with a feather motif in the metalwork. The feathers are a tribute to Chief Nemacolin of the Delawares, guide to George Washington and the resort's namesake.

Design work was in consultation with Hughes Design Associates and Metropolitan Lighting Design Inc. in northern Virginia.

We customized the dimensions of our Olde World glass-arm chandelier design to work in hallways and under lofty ceilings. Olde World is reminiscent of Bohemia, where Schonbek was founded in 1870.

In three months we delivered over 400 crystal wall sconces and chandeliers.

If you have a lighting assignment that's too important to be handled out of a catalog, contact us.

FREE VIDEO "BEYOND LIGHTING": CALL 1.800.836.1892

SCHONBEK®

Schonbek Worldwide Lighting Inc., 61 Industrial Blvd., Plattsburgh NY 12901-1908. Showroom in Dallas TX, by appointment.
Tel: 800 836 1892 or 518 563 7500   Fax: 518 563 4228   email: sales@schonbek.com   Website: www.schonbek.com

Interestingly, customers accept the fact that service can be indifferent or poor in the highly popular "quick-casual" restaurants because they like everything else about being there. It's a sign of how fast these establishments are growing that the relatively low level of training that suffices for quick-service restaurants is not quite sufficient in table-service settings. Nevertheless, consumers like dining out and take-out, and the food service industry is feverishly rolling out new ways to satisfy them.

*H*igh-end or low-end, hoteliers and restaurateurs know the customer will be served no matter what the international economy or the political arena is doing.

High-end or low-end, hoteliers and restaurateurs know the customer will be served no matter what the international economy or the political arena is doing. Not surprisingly, architecture and interior design remain among their most potent techniques for delivering the promises they make to the public about value, convenience and enjoyment. Just stroll through the latest work of the talented hospitality designers who are represented in the pages of Hospitality & Restaurant Design No. 3. The most successful environments serving the hospitality industry truly offer something for everyone.

Roger Yee, an architecture graduate of Yale School of Architecture, has received honors for his work in the field from such organizations as the American Institute of Architects, the American Society of Interior Designers and the Association of Business Publishers. He has been editor-in-chief of Corporate Design & Realty, Contract, and Unique Homes, contributor to Business Week, Engineering News Record and Woman's Day Kitchens & Baths as well as author of Hospitality & Restaurant Design No. 3, Healthcare Spaces No. 1, and Corporate Interiors No. 5.

His other activities in the field have included being marketing advisor to Cushman & Wakefield, a national real estate firm, serving as draftsman and designer to architecture firms, most notably Philip Johnson & John Burgee, and lecturing on design at institutions of higher education, including Dartmouth College and Columbia University. He is a consultant on editorial, public relations and marketing issues to numerous organizations in the design community.

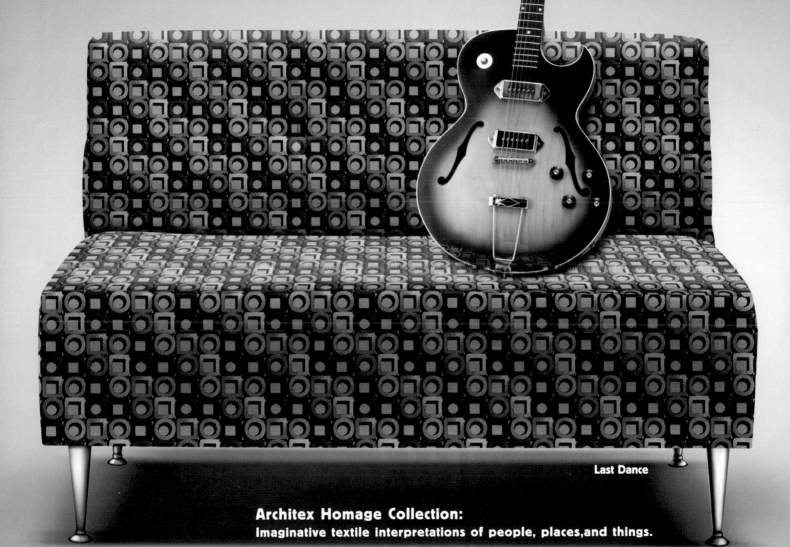

Since my baby left me
I found a new place
to ~~dwell~~. SIT!

Last Dance

Architex Homage Collection:
Imaginative textile interpretations of people, places, and things.

20th Century Influences
Architex®

architex-ljh.com
800.621.0827

Sofa: Retrospect by Carolina
an Architex furniture partner

Project Resources

Ah! Mooré Gourmet Coffee & Bakery
Design firm: URS Corporation

Furniture: Bright Lounge Furniture, Epic Chairs, Sandler Tables
Carpets / Flooring: Atlas
Fabrics: DesignTex, Maharam
Lighting: Belfer, Elliptipar

ARIA at the Fairmont Hotel, Chicago, IL
Design firm: Marve Cooper Design, LLC

Furniture: Design Link, Shelby Williams
Carpets / Flooring: Ann Sacks, Durkan, Stone Source
Fabrics: Cortina Leathers, HBF Textiles, Kravet, Larsen, Pollack, Yves Gonnet
Lighting: Delta, Lightolier
Ceilings: USG
Wallcoverings: Innovations, Koroseal

Bamba!
Design firm: Haverson Architecture & Design P.C.

Furniture: JC Furniture
Carpets / Flooring: DalTile, Prestige Mills, Terrazzo
Fabrics: Carnegie, Douglass Industries, Duralee, Schumacher
Lighting: ABC Carpet, Arte De Mexico, Artesanos, Fairfield Lighting, Lightolier
Ceilings: Benjamin Moore
Wallcoverings: Benjamin Moore

Boca Rio Golf Club
Design firm: Mojo Stumer Associates

Furniture: Dakota Jackson, Pheonix Manufacturers, Todd Hase
Fabrics: Corragio, Donghia, Jim Thompson, Kravet, Nobilis, Osborne & Little, Paul Brayton, Pierre Frey
Lighting: Leucos
Wallcoverings: Garret Leather

Boomtown Casino
Design firm: Earl Swensson Associates, Inc.

Furniture: Shafer
Carpets / Flooring: American Olean Tile, Durkan Custom Carpet
Fabrics: Arc-Com, Momentum
Ceilings: Armstrong

Borgata Hotel Casino & Spa
Design firm: Dougall Design Associates

Furniture: Randolph & Hein, Dakota Jackson, Astoria, Chairmasters, Lewis Mittman/Edward Ferrell, Murray's Iron Works, Troy Wesnidge
Carpets / Flooring: Couristan
Fabrics: Donghia, Edelman Leather, Maharam, Bergamo, Jim Thompson
Lighting: Great Things...and Bob's your Uncle
Sculpture: Dale Chihuly

Brasserie Vert, Hollywood & Highland Center
Design firm: Engstrom Design Group

Furniture: ICF Group, Sandler, Tonon, West Coast Industries
Carpets / Flooring: Architectural Products Group, Daltile, Seneca Tiles
Fabrics: Designtex, 1+1, Knoll
Lighting: Artemide, Lightspann, Sistemalux
Wallcoverings: Arte, Benjamin Moore, Laminart, Wolf Gordon

Broadway Lounge, New York Marriott Marquis, Times Square
Design firm: Arnold Syrop Associates, Architects

Furniture: Delta, Munrod Interiors
Carpets / Flooring: Brinton
Fabrics: ArcCom, Designtex, Frank Bella, Kravet, Maharam, Pallas Textiles
Lighting: Sirmos
Ceilings: USG
Wallcoverings: Nemo Tile

Chattanoogan
Design firm: Looney & Associates

Furniture: Donghia, McGuire, Tex-Style, William Montague
Carpets / Flooring: Innovative
Fabrics: Donghia, Edelman Leather, J. Robert Scott
Lighting: Baldinger Lighting, Charman
Wallcoverings: Innovations, MDC

Chisholm Club, Renaissance Worthington Hotel, Fort Worth, TX
Design firm: Arnold Syrop Associates, Architects

Furniture: Delta, Falcon, Munrod Interiors, Shelby Williams
Fabrics: ArcCom, Brunschwig & Fils, Cortina Leather, Fabricut, Maharam
Lighting: Kane Schrader, Sirmos
Ceilings: USG
Wallcoverings: Modeworks

Clock Lounge, New York Marriott Marquis, Times Square
Design firm: Arnold Syrop Associates, Architects

Furniture: Delta, John Gutierrez
Carpets / Flooring: Edward Fields
Fabrics: ArcCom, Frank Bella, Kravet, Maharam, Schumacher, Zimmer-Rohde
Lighting: Sirmos, Triton Industries

Conrad Bangkok
Design firm: Wilson & Associates

Furniture: Chime Design
Carpets / Flooring: Carpets International
Fabrics: Jim Thompson

Crowne Plaza Universal Hotel
Design firm: Fugleberg Koch Architects

Furniture: Century, DalTile, Kimball Lodging, Shelby Williams
Carpets / Flooring: Atlas, DalTile, Design Weave, Durkan
Fabrics: David Deel Company, Momentum, Paul Brayton, P. Kaufman, S. Harris, Valley Forge
Lighting: Bega, Bernhardt, Corbett Lighting, Davis Miller, D.M. Lighting, Framburg, Kichler Lighting, Light Source, Lite Source, Pacific Coast Contract
Ceilings: Armstrong, MDC, USG
Wallcoverings: Genesys Wallcovering, Innovations, JM Lynne, LSI Laminating Service

WALTERS WICKER

Courtside Club, Los Gatos
Design firm: Orlando Diaz-Azcuy Designs

Furniture: McGuire
Fabrics: Osbourne & Little
Lighting: Boyd
Ceilings: Benjamin Moore
Wallcoverings: Benjamin Moore

Dumont Plaza Hotel
Design firm: DiLeonardo International, Inc.

Furniture: Contrac, Herman Miller, Royal Custom Designs
Carpets / Flooring: Signature Hospitality
Fabrics: DesignTex, Duralee Fabrics, Harris Fabrics, Motif Designs, Valley Forge Fabrics
Lighting: Challenger Lighting, Coronet Lighting, George Kovacs
Wallcoverings: DesignTex

Falling Leaf Lodge; Chautauqua and Fitness Center
Design firm: Cottle Graybeal Yaw Architects

Carpets / Flooring: Masland
Lighting: B-K Lighting, UltraLights

Fiore, Harrah's Shreveport
Design firm: Marnell Architecture

Furniture: HBF, Murray's Ironworks, Shelby Williams, Westwood Interiors
Carpets / Flooring: Couristan
Fabrics: Jim Thompson Silk, Kravet, Old World Weavers, Osbourne & Little, Quadrille
Lighting: Triton
Wallcoverings: Anya Larkin, Blumenthal, Maya Romanoff, Schumacher

Fogo de Chao
Design firm: Marve Cooper Design, LLC

Furniture: Shelby Williams
Carpets / Flooring: American Olean, Atlas, Stone Design
Fabrics: Maharam

Four Seasons Hotel Cairo at the First Residence
Design firm: Wilson & Associates

Furniture: Pindler & Pindler, R. Jones
Carpets / Flooring: Couristan
Fabrics: Pollack, Silk Dynasty
Lighting: Asfour Crystal, Galleries Odeon
Wallcoverings: Peter Gorman Studios

Fullerton Hotel, Singapore
Design firm: HBA/Hirsch Bedner Associates

Furniture: Axis Collection, Bradbury Collection, Cheng Meng, City Studio, Donghia, Jiwa Asia, Michael Berman, Michael Rudin, Nancy Corzine, Therien
Carpets / Flooring: Brintons, Tascot Templeton, Walker Zangar
Lighting: Boyd, Distant Origin, Donghia Lighting, Flos USA, HRS, Hwang Bishop, Ingo Maurer, Richardo Lighting, Sirmos
Wallcoverings: Goodrich Wallcoverings & Carpets, Maya Romanoff

Grand Resort Lagonissi
Design firm: DiLeonardo International, Inc.

Lighting: Fine Art Lamps, Linge Roset

Grand Hyatt Tampa Bay
Design firm: Looney & Associates

Furniture: Marquis, William Montague
Carpets / Flooring: Atlas, Signature
Fabrics: Kravet, P/Kaufman, Valley Forge
Lighting: Sirmos
Wallcoverings: MDC, Metro Wallcovering

Harrah's Bayview Tower
Design firm: Marnell Architecture

Furniture: Baker, Hickory Chair, Kindel, Newman Frey, Westwood Interiors
Carpets / Flooring: Brintons, Decorative Carpets
Fabrics: Brunschwig et Fils, Clarence House, Donghia, Glant, S. Harris
Lighting: Boyd, Nancy Corzine, Nessen, Triton
Ceilings: Savoy Studios
Wallcoverings: Anya Larkin, Edelman Leather, Innovations, Winfield, Wolf Gordon

Hilton Club New York
Design firm: SFA Design

Furniture: Lambert, Royal Custom
Carpets / Flooring: Milliken, Templeton
Fabrics: Kravet, Valley Forge
Lighting: Coronet, Hallmark, Scott Lamps
Wallcoverings: Metro Wallcovering

Hilton Suites Dallas North
Design firm: Earl Swensson Associates, Inc.

Furniture: AGI, Bernhardt, Century, Chaircraft, HBF, Hickory Chair, Lay-Z-Boy, Lowenstein, Nevins, Stone Line, Sunbrella, Teknion, Thomasville, Tropitone, Vaughn, Woodard
Carpets / Flooring: Amtico, Crossville Ceramics, DalTile, Mannington, Shaw, Templeton
Fabrics: Arc-Com, Architex, Fabric UT, Knoll
Lighting: Hallmark, North Bay, Sun Valley, Tec Lighting, Visa
Ceilings: Armstrong
Wallcoverings: JM Lynne, Knoll Textiles

Horsley Bridge International, London
Design firm: Orlando Diaz-Azcuy Designs

Furniture: HBF, Herman Miller, Knoll
Carpets / Flooring: Pacific Crest Mills
Fabrics: Fortuny, HBF
Lighting: Leucos

Jasper's Legacy Center
Design firm: Engstrom Design Group

Furniture: Brown Jordan, Design Link International, Loewenstein, Fong Brothers, West Coast Industries
Carpets / Flooring: American Slate Company, Armstrong, Daltile, Kurkan Commercial, Heath, Johnsonite, McIntyre Tile
Fabrics: DesignTex, DuraleeKnoll, Maharam, Momentum, Pollack, Valley Forge
Lighting: Capri, CP Lighting, Lightspann
Wallcoverings: Abet Laminati, Arte, Benjamin Moore, Blumenthal, Contract Wallcoverings, Nevamar, Pionite, Sherwin Williams

Keefer's
Design firm: Aria Group Architects

Carpets / Flooring: Terrazo
Lighting: Juno, Metalux
Ceilings: USG

Junior's Grand Central Station
Design firm: Haverson Architecture & Design P.C.

Carpets / Flooring: Terrazzo
Lighting: Poulsen Lighting
Ceilings: Armstrong, Benjamin Moore
Wallcoverings: Benjamin Moore, DalTile

J.W. Marriott Hotel, Miami, FL
Design firm: Daroff Design Inc.

Furniture: Astoria, Baker, Bevan Funnell, Beverly, Century, Chairmasters, Gregson, Hendredon, Hickory Chair, LaBarge, Lane, Mark David, Murray's Iron Works, Paul Brayton, Royal Custom Designs, Shelby Williams, Steelcase, Wood & Hogan
Carpets / Flooring: Century, Durkan, Karastan Bigelow, Sewelson, Templeton Carpet, Ulster Carpet
Fabrics: Architex, Bergamo, Brunschwig & Fils, Cortina Leathers, Cowtan & Tout, DesignTex, Edelman Leather, JM Lynne, Kravet, Lee Jofa, Maharam, Old World Weavers, Paul Brayton, Quadrille, Scalamandre Contract, Spectrum Fabrics, Spinneybeck, Stroheim & Romann, Valley Forge Fabrics
Lighting: Chapman Lighting, Fine Art Lamps, International Ironworks, Remington, Stiffel
Wallcoverings: BlumenthalEssex Wallcovering, Gilford, Koroseal, MDC, Victrex, WolfGordon

Katzenberg's Express
Design firm: Haverson Architecture & Design P.C.

Furniture: Empire, Formica, L&B
Fabrics: Maharam
Lighting: Eureka, Lightolier
Ceilings: Scuffmaster, Wolf Gordon, Zolatone
Wallcoverings: Benjamin Moore, JM Lynne, Scuffmaster, Wolf Gordon, Zolatone

Kona Grill
Design firm: Aria Group Architects, Inc.

Furniture: EJ Industries, Loewenstein, Luc WI
Carpets / Flooring: American Slate Company, Atlas Carpets
Fabrics: Momentum Textiles
Lighting: Halo, Neidhardt, Vise Lighting
Ceilings: McNichols, USG
Wallcoverings: Innovations

Le Touessrok Hotel & Spa, Mauritius
Design firm: HBA/Hirsch Bedner Associates

Carpets / Flooring: Silver Brook Quartzite
Fabrics: Old World Weavers, Pierre Frey, Pollack, Scalamandre, Silk Trading, Sunbrella
Lighting: Taller Uno

Malliouhana Spa
Design firm: Earl Swensson Associates, Inc.

Furniture: Brown Jordan, Palecek
Carpets / Flooring: DalTile
Wallcoverings: DalTile

Marriott Hotel Orlando - Lake Mary
Design firm: Jonathan Nehmer + Associates, Inc.

Furniture: Pedley Furniture
Carpets / Flooring: Shaw Carpet, Ulster Carpets
Fabrics: Valley Forge
Ceilings: USG
Wallcoverings: Versa Wallcovering

Masa's Restaurant
Design firm: Orlando Diaz-Azcuy Designs

Carpets / Flooring: Pacific Crest
Fabrics: Cowtan & Tout, HBF
Ceilings: Eurospan by Wall Technology
Wallcoverings: Benjamin Moore

Matthew's Restaurant
Design firm: Rink Reynolds Diamond Fisher Wilson P.A.

Furniture: Falcon, Loewenstein
Carpets / Flooring: Mannington
Fabrics: DesignTex, Donghia, Sina Pearson
Lighting: Leucos, Louis Poulsen, Tech Lighting
Ceilings: USG
Wallcoverings: Benjamin Moore, Maya Romanoff

Milwaukee Road Depot
Design firm: Elness Swenson Graham Architects Inc.

Furniture: Royal custom, Uttermost
Carpets / Flooring: Armstrong, DalTile, Durkan, Shaw
Fabrics: Arc-Com, Momentum
Lighting: Fine Arts
Ceilings: USG
Wallcoverings: JM Lynne, Maharam, Seabrook, VWC

MoMo's Restaurant
Design firm: MBH Architects

Furniture: Agnes Bourne, Lowenstein, Shafer
Carpets / Flooring: DalTile, Walker Zanger
Fabrics: Donghia, Edelman leather, Jack Lenor Larsen, Old World Weavers
Wallcoverings: Clearance House

Nashville Marriott at Vanderbilt University
Design firm: Di Leonardo International, Inc.

Furniture: Chairmaster, David Edward, Lane, Murray's Ironworks, William Switzer
Carpets / Flooring: Brinton's
Fabrics: Arc-Con, S. Harris, Swavelle/Mill Creek Fabrics, Valley Forge Fabrics
Lighting: George Kovacs, Illuminating Experiences, Inc., Scott Lamp Co., Unilight
Wallcoverings: U.S. Vinyl

Newport Coast Villas
Design firm: MBH Architects

Furniture: Fong Brothers
Carpets / Flooring: Couristan
Fabrics: Kravet, Pindler & Pindler, S. Harris
Lighting: International Ironworks

Nyla at the Dylan Hotel
Design firm: Haverson Architecture & Design P.C.

Furniture: JC Furniture, L&B
Fabrics: Kravet, Maharam, Majilite
Lighting: Hubbardon Forge, Metalarte, Van Teal Lighting
Ceilings: Scalamandre

Pacific Athletic Club, San Diego
Design firm: Orlando Diaz-Azcuy Design

Furniture: McGuire
Carpets / Flooring: Abbey Carpets
Fabrics: HBF

Panevino ristorante & Gourmet Deli
Design firm: Marnell Architecture

Furniture: Charter, Guy Chaddock, MTS, Powell Cabinets, Shelby Williams
Carpets / Flooring: Brintons, Scott Group
Fabrics: Architex, Liz Jordan Hill for DesignTex, Maharam, Osbourne & Little, P/Kaufman
Lighting: Lightspan, Ralph Lauren, Studio Metz, 2000 Degrees
Ceilings: Natural Cork
Wallcoverings: Bizazza Tile, Scalamandre

Park Towers
Design firm: SFA Design

Furniture: Anvil Furniture, Jenson Custom, Mission Custom
Carpets / Flooring: US Axminister Carpets
Fabrics: Kneidler Fauchere, Kravet, Randolph & Hein, Rose Tarlow
Lighting: Anvil Lighting

P.F. Chang's Chinese Bistro
Design firm: Aria Group Architects, Inc.

Furniture: E.J. Industries, Falcon Products, Shafer, Woodard
Carpets / Flooring: American Slate, Junckers Wood Flooring, World Wide Stone
Fabrics: Boltaflex, DesignTex, Maharam
Ceilings: Owens Corning
Wallcoverings: Ann sacks, Koroseal, Pionite, Pratt & Lambert, Seabrook Contract

P.F. Chang's China Bistro
Design firm: MBH Architects

Furniture: Chairmasters, EJ Industries, Falcon Products, Pionite, Shafer, Wilsonart, Woodard
Carpets / Flooring: American Slate, Atlas, DalTile, Flor Gres Tile, Roppe Rubber Tile, Spazi Tile, Stonecraft Industries
Fabrics: Boltaflex Fabrics, Britex Fabrics, Donghia, Fabricut Contract, Gretchen Bellinger, Pollack, Rose Brand
Lighting: Maya Romanoff, USG Interiors
Wallcoverings: Marlite, Maya Romanoff, Pratt & Lambert

Ponte Vedra Inn & Club
Design firm: Rink Reynolds Diamond Fisher Wilson P.A.

Furniture: Beachley, Collection Reproduction, Milling Road, MTS, Pierce Martin, Sterling
Carpets / Flooring: Durkan
Fabrics: Architex, Bergamo, Dazian, DesignTex, Kravet, Lee Jofa, Maharam, Old World Weavers, Pindler & Pindler, Rodolph, Scalamandre, Travers, Westgate
Lighting: Artemide, Eureka, Fad Lighting, Fine Art Lamps, Flos USA, Ironware International, Nessen, Tech Lighting
Ceilings: USG
Wallcoverings: Benjamin Moore, DalTile, nevamar, Seabrook

Radisson Hotel at Carlson Park
Design firm: Elness Swenson Graham Architects Inc.

Furniture: Bauer International, D'Style, Lane, Lexington, Murray's Iron Works, Shelby Williams, Tropitone, Troy Wesnige, Wells Industries, Woodard
Carpets / Flooring: DalTile, Karastan, Milliken, Westweave
Fabrics: Fabricut Contract, Majilite, Moore & Giles, Pindler & Pindler
Lighting: Corbet Lighting, Coronet, Fine Art Lamps, Light Group Industries, Seagull
Ceilings: Armstrong, USG
Wallcoverings: Blumenthal, JM Lynne, Koroseal, Versa

Radisson Plaza VII
Design firm: SFA Design

Furniture: Fleetwood, Integra
Carpets / Flooring: Milliken
Fabrics: Delta, Valley Forge
Lighting: Coronet
Wallcoverings: Metro, Seller & Josephson

Let Us Show You Our "Value"able Side

kravetcontract

Phone: 888.891.4112   Fax: 800.367.9026   www.kravetcontract.com

Restaurant Medure
Design firm: Rink Reynolds Diamond Fisher Wilson P.A.

Furniture: Davis, Hafele, Peter Pepper
Carpets / Flooring: Interface
Fabrics: Arpel, Dazian, MTS
Lighting: Lightolier
Ceilings: USG
Wallcoverings: Benjamin Moore

restaurant rm
Design firm: Haverson Architecture and Design P.C.

Fabrics: Clarence House, Henry Calvin, Maharam, Schumacher
Lighting: Bruck Lighting, Lee's Studio, Shefts, Spero Lighting
Wallcoverings: Benjamin Moore

Rio Palazzo Suites
Design firm: Marnell Architecture

Furniture: Baker, Charter, Karges, Kindel, Nancy Corzine, Quatrain, Randolph & Flein
Fabrics: Bergamo, Brunschweig et Fils, Clarence House, Old World Weavers, Scalamandre, Schumacher
Lighting: Cedric Hartman, Nancy Corzine, Panache, Triton
Wallcoverings: Anya Larkin, Maya Romanoff

Ritz-Carlton Bachelor Gulch Hotel
Design firm: Wilson & Associates

Furniture: A. Rudin, Artifact, Baker, Bausman, Gorsrich, Milling Road, Therien & Co.
Fabrics: Abraded Leather, Eliot & Assoc., Moore & Giles, Ralph Lauren
Lighting: Allan Knight, Bouyea, Functional Metal, Originals 22

Rosewood Hotel at the Al-Faisaliah Complex
Design firm: Di Leonardo International, Inc.

Furniture: Artistic Frame, Baker, Beverly Furniture, Chairmasters, Donghia Furniture & Textiles, Interior Crafts, Jeffco Enterprises, Mirak, Inc.
Fabrics: Arc-Com, Clarence House Fabrics, Cortina Leather, DesignTex, Edelman Leather, HBF, Kravets Fabrics, Paul Brayton, Robert Allen, Scalamandre, Sina Pearson, Travers
Lighting: Luce, Panoramic Architectural Products, Sirros
Wallcoverings: Kravet

Royal Pacific Resort at Universal Orlando
Design firm: Fugleberg Koch Architects

Carpets / Flooring: Azrock-VCT, DalTile, Illster, Shaw, Templeton
Fabrics: Kravet

Rumba
Design firm: Aria Group Architects, Inc.

Carpets / Flooring: American Olean, Junkers Wood Flooring
Fabrics: Arc-Com, Donghia, Maharam
Lighting: Chista, Rainbow Lighting

Smith & Wollensky - Easton Town Center
Design firm: Haverson Architecture & Design P.C.

Furniture: JC Furniture, L&B
Carpets / Flooring: Armstrong, DalTile, Harmil Carpets, Stone Source
Fabrics: Duralee, Kravet, Majilite, Nanik, Robert Allen Contract, Sunbrella
Lighting: Fairfield Lighting, Lightolier, Spectrum Lighting, Urban Archeology
Ceilings: Armstrong, Benjamin Moore
Wallcoverings: American Decorative Ceilings, Benjamin Moore, DalTile, Stone Source

Spa at the Hotel Hershey
Design firm: Earl Swensson Associates, Inc.

Furniture: Hickory Chair, Milling Road
Carpets / Flooring: Brintons, Crossville Ceramics, Perma Grain
Fabrics: Arc-Com, Architex, Schumacher
Lighting: Metropolitan
Wallcoverings: Greeff, Hastings Tile

Spago Four Seasons Resort at the Four Seasons Maui at Wailea
Design firm: Engstrom Design Group

Furniture: Asiatix, Bernhardt, Brown Jordan, Design Link International, Krug, West Coast Industries
Carpets / Flooring: Ann Sacks, Daltile, Shaw Contract
Fabrics: DesignTex, Maharam, Pollack, Rodolph, Unika Vaev
Lighting: Luz Lampcraft, Mark Harvey
Ceilings: USG
Wallcoverings: Blumenthal, Chemetal, JM Lynne, Maharam, Pionite, Sherwin Williams, Silk Dynasty, Wilsonart, Winfield Design Associates

St. Regis Shanghai, China
Design firm: HBA/Hirsch Bedner Associates

Carpets / Flooring: Taiping Carpet
Fabrics: Andrew Muirhead & Son, ArcCom, Brentano, Jagtar & Sons, Pallas, Teddy & Arthur Edelman
Wallcoverings: Pallas

Sushi Bar and Atrium Function Space, New York Marriott Marquis, Times Square
Design firm: Arnold Syrop Associates, Architects

Furniture: Allermuir, Delta, Shelby Williams
Carpets / Flooring: Brinton, DalTile
Fabrics: Maharam, Pierre Frey, S. Harris, Unika Vaev
Lighting: Luminary Tools
Ceilings: USG

Villas & Spa at Little Dix Bay
Design firm: Wilson & Associates

Furniture: Signature
Fabrics: Barbara Beckman, Crezana, Osborne & Little, Perennials
Lighting: Marianne Jamison
Wallcoverings: Smith & Noble

CALL 888-448-7878 FOR FAST DELIVERY!

We deliver fast, fresh, and hot in 24 hours.

It's that fast. With Bookends, from Shaw Hospitality, your
sample is in your hands in about 24 hours. You can choose
from a wide selection of toppings. That is, you choose the
colors and patterns that you want, and we'll make it and
ship it out pronto. And of course, we'll hold the anchovies.
Bookends. It's fast and fresh to you.

shaw | HOSPITALITY

A Berkshire Hathaway Company

Contact us today at 888-448-7878, online at www.shawinc.com ©2003 SHAW, A Berkshire Hathaway Company

Virginia Crossings Conference Resort
Design firm: Jonathan Nehmer + Associates, Inc.

Furniture: American of Martinsville, Century, Lexington, Southwood
Carpets / Flooring: Milliken, Signature Carpet
Fabrics: Ametex Contract Fabrics, Culp Hospitality, Duralee, Kravet, Robert Allen

Weston Riverwalk
Design firm: Looney & Associates

Furniture: Newman-Frey, R. Jones, William Montague
Carpets / Flooring: Brintons, Innovative
Fabrics: Cappaggio, Edelman Leather, Pollack
Lighting: Newman-Frey
Wallcoverings: JM Lynne, Maya Romanoff

Wolfgang Puck Express Prototype, Coral Spring Center
Design firm: Engstrom Design Group

Furniture: Design Link, Leland, Stua (DWR), West Coast Industries, Westin Neilsen
Carpets / Flooring: Ceramic Tile Designs, Daltile, Italics, McIntryre Tile Co.
Fabrics: DesignTex, Majilite
Ceilings: Armstrong
Wallcoverings: Abet Laminati, Benjamin Moore, Corian, DesignTex, JM Lynne, Innovations, Nevamar, Wilsonart, Wolf Gordon

Woodlands Waterway Marriott
Design firm: Looney & Associates

Furniture: Roy Thomas, Robert Cole, Troy Weinridge
Carpets / Flooring: Anne Sacks, Clayton Miller, Innovative Carpets
Fabrics: Duralee, Kravet, Larsen
Lighting: Baldinger Lighting, International Ironworks, Sirmos
Ceilings: Armstrong
Wallcoverings: JM Lynne, Metro Wallcovering

Wyndham Orlando Resort
Design firm: Jonathan Nehmer + Associates, Inc.

Furniture: Charles Keath, Contract Resources, ERG Corporate, Lambert, Lane, Loewenstein, Mark David, Shelby Williams, Thomasville, Woodard
Carpets / Flooring: Crossville Ceramics, DalTile, Durkan, Masland, Merit, Tarkett Commercial, Templeton
Fabrics: Architex, Braemore Textiles, Charles Samuelson, DesignTex, Kravet, La Fabrique, P/Kaufman, Richloom, Richmond Textiles, Robert Allen, Valley Forge
Lighting: Baldinger Lighting, Contract Resources, Genesis, Illuminating Experiences, Illuminations, Juno, Murray Feiss, Nulco, Pacific Coast Light, Quoizel, Visa Lighting
Ceilings: Armstrong, USG
Wallcoverings: Benjamin Moore, DalTile, Duroplex, Imperial, Tretford, Walltalkers

In the Seat of the Night.

Union League Club
Chicago, Illinois

COLOR

HAMMERED SILVER {SW 2840}

Idle Max Chandelier

NeoCon® SHOWS

NeoCon® Shows

NeoCon® World's Trade Fair

IIDEX®/ NeoCon® Canada

NeoCon® East

NeoCon® West

North America's largest collection of expositions and conferences for interior design and facilities management ...

NeoCon® World's Trade Fair
June 14-16, 2004
The Merchandise Mart • Chicago, Ill.

NeoCon® West
March 25-26, 2004
L.A. Mart®
Los Angeles, Calif.

IIDEX®/NeoCon® Canada
September 30-October 1, 2004
The National Trade Centre
Toronto, Ont.

NeoCon® East
October 7-8, 2004
Baltimore Convention Center
Baltimore, Md.

www.merchandisemart.com 800.677.6278

The Visual Reference Library

of Architecture and Design

American Graphic Design Awards
Cafe Design
Cafes & Coffee Shops
Callison; Creating Smaller Places
Contemporary Exhibit Design
Corporate Interiors
Designing the World's Best Exhibits
Designing the World's Best Supermarkets
Educational Environments
Entertainment Destinations
Entertainment Dining
Gourmet & Specialty Shops
Healthcare Spaces
Hospitality & Restaurant Design
Hot Graphics USA
Indonesian Accents
Point of Purchase Design Annual
Storefronts & Facades
Stores of the Year
Store Windows
Streetscapes
Urban Spaces
Winning Shopping Center Designs

www.visualreference.com

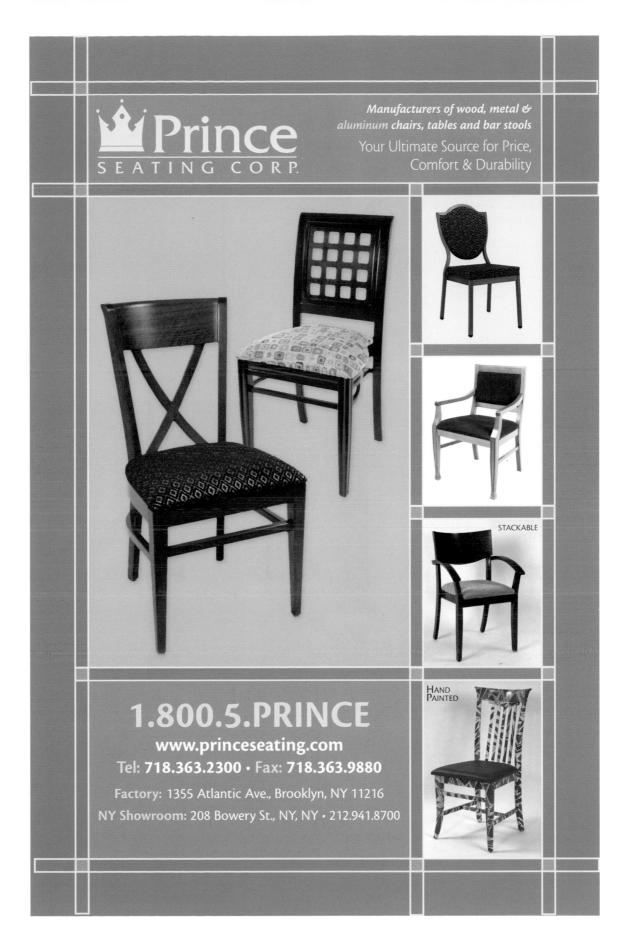

Prince
SEATING CORP.

Manufacturers of wood, metal & aluminum chairs, tables and bar stools
Your Ultimate Source for Price, Comfort & Durability

STACKABLE

HAND PAINTED

1.800.5.PRINCE
www.princeseating.com
Tel: **718.363.2300** • Fax: **718.363.9880**

Factory: 1355 Atlantic Ave., Brooklyn, NY 11216
NY Showroom: 208 Bowery St., NY, NY • 212.941.8700

Advertisers Index

By Jillian Van Dresser

Who's driving hospitality design today?

The hospitality design profession has a long tradition of serving hotel owners and professional hoteliers in shaping the environments for their properties. In the past, an owner knew the appropriate design for his or her property, and engaged a designer to create an appropriate visual image and comfort to define the hotel based on his or her perspective. Clients with multiple hotels often established group standards for consistency. Yet even then, the touch and feel of a hotel was historically dictated by a hotelier. Today, we are increasingly directed by financial and business minds not entrenched in the historical experience of our industry.

Hotels and restaurants are now developed with a different set of criteria and a fresh perspective that sets the stage for creativity. We initiate the creative process by first defining the purpose of our design: Is it bottom line driven, comfort driven, or high profile or market pacer driven? Is it geared to a defined client profile? Or is it a simple clean-up for resale? The answers are as varied as the structures of the financial deals supporting them. But, what the hospitality industry openly shares with designers today is the marketing plan, clearly defined with target markets and guest expectations.

Creativity then comes into play in the form of redefinition. Owners, architects, designers and product manufacturers are providing environments that increasingly elevate hotel guests' exposure to technology, luxury and lifestyles. Right brains and left brains are engaged. The advancement of transportation and information technology has expanded our exposure to the world and its riches providing unending stimuli. Ideas are exchanged globally and our need for continuing education is paramount as hotels provide milieus that offer technological comforts in visually textural settings.

And what is the underpinning that connects a beautiful environment with profitability, with exceeding guests' expectations, with being an industry leader, or with enjoying a comfortable place in a market? Quite simply and most importantly, it is service. The talent of visionary design professionals today is exceptional, and the projects that we admire in this publication are a clear demonstration of their ability to create built environments that are very distinctive for our guests. Nevertheless, we must look to our hoteliers and their knowledge of service to create the final guest experience--an experience that ensures our guests feel special in hotels created just for them.

Jillian Van Dresser is National President of the Network of Executive Women in Hospitality (NEWH, Inc.) and principal of The Van Dresser Company in Atlanta.

284

emeco

Index by Projects